Sleep *and*
Dreams

Sleep and Dreams

Andrew T. McPhee

FRANKLIN WATTS
A Division of Grolier Publishing
New York • London • Hong Kong • Sydney
Danbury, Connecticut

There, that is our secret: go to sleep!
You will wake, and remember, and understand.
　　　　　　　　　—Elizabeth Barrett Browning

Note to readers: Definitions for words in **bold** type can be found in the Glossary at the back of this book.

Interior design by Molly Heron
Cover photographs ©: Stone: mountains; The Image Works: water lilies, flute; all others courtesy of Photodisc, Inc.

Photographs ©: A.T. McPhee: 10; Dembinsky Photo Assoc.: 28 (Dan Dempster), 32 right (Bruce Montagne), 72 (NovaStock); Liaison Agency, Inc.: 37 (Michelle Barnes), 87 (Gerhard Hinterleitner/Contrast), 15 (Wolfgang Käehler), 32 left (Zillioux); PhotoEdit: 70 (Tony Freeman), 64 (Phil McCarten), 81 (National Library of Medicine), 46 (David Young-Wolff); Stock Boston: 51 (Elizabeth Crews), 18 (Grant LeDuc), 60 (Peter Menzel); Stone: 39 (Anthony Marsland), 14 (Thomas Peterson), 43 (Richard Stock); Visuals Unlimited: 75 (David Sieren), 19 (SIU).

Illustrations by Mike DiGiorgio

Visit Franklin Watts on the Internet at:
http://publishing.grolier.com

Library of Congress Cataloging-in-Publication Data

McPhee, Andrew T.
　　Sleep and dreams / by Andrew T. McPhee
　　　　p. cm.
　　Includes bibliographical references and index.
　　Summary: Discusses the nature of sleep and dreams, the causes of and treatments for sleep disorders, and the possible meaning of common dreams.
　　ISBN 0-531-11735-9 (lib. bdg.)
　　1. Sleep—Juvenile literature. 2. Dreams—Juvenile literature. [1. Sleep. II. Dreams.] I. Title.

QP425.M377　　　2001
616.8'21—dc21　　00-028971

ACKNOWLEDGMENTS

This book would not have been possible without the love and support of my wonderful wife Gay. She spent far too many hours looking at the back of my head as I pounded away at the keyboard. I am grateful for her consistent encouragement and understanding. Thank you, my love. This one's for you.

CONTENTS

The Mysterious World of Sleep and Dreams

My son Joshua can sleep anywhere, anytime. My wife and I have pictures of him sleeping in all sorts of strange places and positions. One photo shows him asleep under some seats in a busy auditorium. Another shows him sleeping soundly on the bottom shelf of a bookcase. In yet another photo, Joshua is kneeling in a chair, his forehead against the armrest, fast asleep in what looks like a most uncomfortable position!

We sleep so much that you might think we would all be experts on the subject. But that's not the case. No other natural condition is experienced so often and understood so poorly. Sleep is such a mystery that even scientists have difficulty defining it clearly.

Sleep is a natural condition of the body. While sleeping, you are not aware of your surroundings. When you fall asleep, you don't see the light in the hallway, hear the sound of the wind rustling the curtains, or sense the softness of the sheets surrounding your body. You might be awakened by an alarm clock, a radio, or perhaps a parent calling your name from the breakfast table. For most people, this simple cycle of being awake, falling

Four-year-old Joshua Marchetti of Doylestown, Pennsylvania, can sleep anywhere. Children his age sleep more than teenagers or adults.

asleep, and then being awake again repeats itself every day of every week of every month for a lifetime.

Most people spend about 33 percent of their life sleeping. That means you spend one-third of your life doing something you probably don't know or remember much about. But although you might not remember much about it, sleep is an enormously important part of life. It is so important, in fact, that you can't survive without it.

Joshua's ability to fall asleep almost anywhere intrigues me. For most people, including Joshua, sleep comes easily and brings much needed rest. For others, sleep is elusive. It lurks in the shadows. Questions about sleep fill the night for these people. Why can't I sleep? What can I do to fall asleep more easily? Why do I always feel tired during the day even though I think I slept so well?

These are just a few of the mysteries of sleep. Come along as we unravel each one.

Chapter 1

The Biology of Sleep

If you think about it, very few things in life are absolutely necessary for survival. You can live without medical care, though you probably wouldn't live as well or as long. You can live without a car or a minivan—people walked or rode horses for hundreds of years before Henry Ford invented the Model-T. You can live without that really cool sweater you saw at the mall, although you probably didn't think so when you first saw it in the store window. But you can't survive without oxygen to breathe, water, food—and sleep. Sleep is that important.

Sleep gives your body something it can't get when you're awake—deep, penetrating rest. Sleep recharges cells throughout the body and prepares them for the next day's activities. A special chemical called **melatonin** produced during sleep gives a boost to the body's **immune system**, which fights infections. Melatonin also blocks some viruses from causing infection and may help to prevent certain tumors from forming.

Sleep helps your body's cells grow and repair themselves. During sleep, the body stores energy it will use later. Some researchers believe that dreams, which occur during sleep, help strengthen memories and sort out emotions. That's an impressive list of benefits for such a seemingly simple activity.

Sleep and Animals

You've probably seen animals sleep. Dogs, cats, parakeets, and hawks sleep. Rabbits, guinea pigs, and most other kinds of household pets also sleep. Some animals don't sleep. These include invertebrates such as insects, sea jellies, and lobsters. Cold-blooded vertebrates such as snakes and lizards rest periodically throughout the day, but they don't sleep either—at least not in the same way that birds and mammals do. Many fish species spend long periods of time without moving. Whether they're actually sleeping or just resting is a mystery scientists haven't yet solved.

House cats sleep more than 12 hours a day. Maybe these cats are resting up for a midnight romp through the living room!

Some animals sleep a great deal each day. The giant sloth and many species of bats sleep as many as 20 hours a day. Lions, tigers, and other big cats sleep about 17 hours a day, snoozing through an amazing 70 percent of their lives. House cats typically sleep more than 12 hours a day.

Giant sloths sleep about 20 hours a day.

Most animals that sleep for long periods each day are predators—animals that survive by hunting and killing other animals. Predators at the top of the food chain often sleep for long periods of time since they don't have to remain alert. After all, who would wake an 800-pound (363-kilogram) grizzly bear?

Prey animals—animals that are hunted and eaten by other animals—spend considerably less time sleeping. That makes sense because they have to watch out for predators. Cows, sheep, goats, and other plant-eating animals sleep in fits and starts. Giraffes sleep only about 2 hours a day. Horses sleep about 3 hours a day.

Some birds—particularly those that travel great distances—may sleep during flight. Perching birds, such as chickadees and blue jays, usually sleep standing up. Their leg and claw muscles remain tense while they sleep so they don't suddenly fall off their perch.

Perhaps the most unusual sleep behavior among animals is unihemispheric sleep, in which half of the animal's brain falls asleep while the other half remains alert. Scientists studying dolphins in the Black Sea found that the animals engaged in this half-and-half form of sleep. After about 4 hours, the sleeping side of the dolphin's brain awakens and the previously alert side falls asleep. This allows the dolphin to remain constantly alert but still get some rest.

Ducks in a Row

Ducks also experience unihemispheric sleep. Researchers at Indiana State University in Terre Haute, Indiana, studied sleep behavior in caged ducks lined up in rows of four. They found that the ducks at the ends of the row spent more than twice as much time in unihemispheric sleep as did the two center ducks.

The middle ducks probably sensed that they were safe from predators because they were shielded on either side by another duck. The ducks on the ends, though, probably sensed that they were more open to attack, so they remained more alert than their inside neighbors. The end ducks slept with one eye open, and rotated their bodies in the water so that their open eye was looking toward the areas from which a predator might attack.

In humans, the entire brain falls asleep. We pass from being awake to being asleep within seconds. In one study, scientists taped the eyelids of research subjects open. Then they asked the subjects to press a button each time a bright light flashed in front of their eyes. The scientists wanted to find out whether the flashing lights interfered with sleep.

For the first 10 or 15 minutes, each subject pressed the button every time the light flashed. Then the buttons fell silent. The flashing lights didn't keep sleep away, even when the eyelids were open!

It's Just a Stage

In human beings, the five stages of sleep occur more or less in sequence. This sequence may repeat itself several times a night. During Stage 1 sleep, you're no longer aware of what's happening around you. You may feel as if you're floating—peaceful, at rest, and calm. Your muscles are relaxed, your eyelids are closed, and your heart rate and breathing become slow and regular. Your temperature drops too. As that happens, you might pull the covers closer to your chin.

You can be easily awakened during Stage 1 sleep. The barking of a dog, the sudden loudness of a late-night commercial, or someone whispering, "Come on, it's time for bed," may be enough to wake you. You won't be fully awake though. You'll feel groggy, and your muscles will feel sluggish because they're so relaxed.

During this light, relaxing level of sleep, the amount of electrical activity in your brain changes, as it does in every stage of sleep. Scientists measure electrical activity in the brain using a machine called an **electroencephalograph**. The machine senses tiny electrical changes given off by the activity of nerve cells in the brain and records them on an **electroencephalogram (EEG).**

Different types of cell activity make different brain-wave patterns on an EEG. When you're awake and your brain cells are very active, your EEG reading shows a lot of small, rapid waves. Scientists call these **beta waves.** These occur at a rate of at least 15 waves per second. During Stage 1 sleep, brain-wave activity slows. At this time, your EEG shows **alpha waves,** which occur at a rate of only 8 to 10 waves per second. Alpha waves are highly

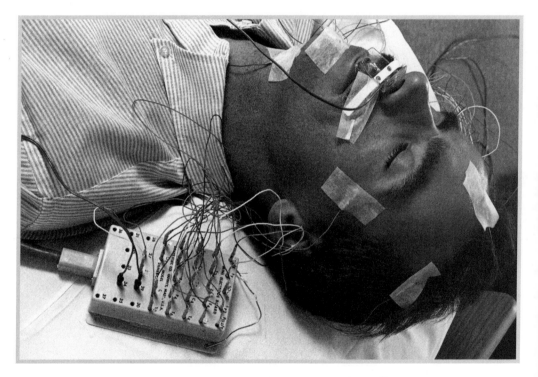

This man is having an electroencephalogram, a recording of brain waves. The wires pick up electrical signals from his brain and send them to a recording device. Doctors use the recordings to learn more about brain activity.

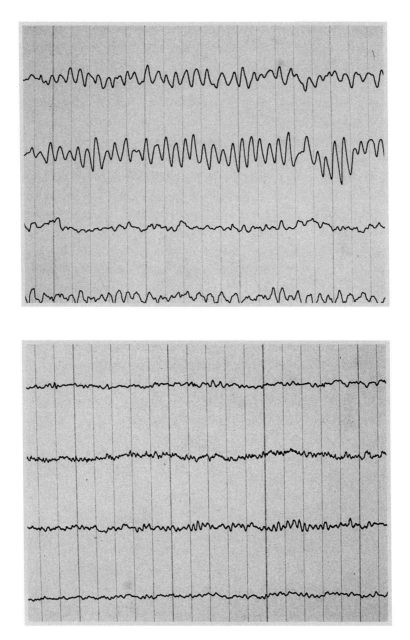

These typical alpha waves (top) and beta waves (bottom) were recorded using an electroencephalograph.

regular and have sharp spikes, much like the teeth on a comb. If your eyes open or if something disturbs your rest, alpha waves disappear immediately.

If you're not awakened from Stage 1 sleep, you enter **Stage 2 sleep.** In this stage, you sleep right through loud commercials. It becomes difficult to wake you. Sudden muscle contractions may jerk your arm or leg. An EEG of your brain waves during this stage shows deeper, slower brain waves, called **theta waves.** Your eyes may open and move from side to side at this time, but you won't see anything. Your blood pressure drops during Stage 2 sleep, and your temperature continues to fall. Together, the first two stages of sleep usually last about 30 minutes.

Stage 3 sleep is a short transition phase that occurs just before **Stage 4 sleep**, also called **delta sleep** or **deep sleep.** Stages 3 and 4 are characterized by a period of total calm and comfort. At this time, you're completely unaware of the world around you. Your brain waves become even slower, and your heart rate becomes more regular. Your blood pressure continues to drop. You don't sweat or shiver during deep sleep, no matter how hot or cold you might be. An EEG taken during deep sleep shows very large, slow brain waves called **delta waves.**

A child in delta sleep can be picked up, changed into pajamas, carried to bed, and kissed goodnight without waking up. Only a major disturbance—a fire alarm, for example—will wake someone from delta sleep.

If something wakes you from this deep sleep, you'll feel slow and foggy at first. It may take a while before you feel fully awake and alert. Firefighters, paramedics, police officers, and other people who need to respond quickly to emergencies can train themselves to wake from deep sleep more quickly than other people, but even these people need several minutes to wake up completely.

Scientists consider deep sleep the most restful sleep possible. This is the time when the body renews itself. Energy levels rebuild and the body becomes refreshed and ready for the next day's activities. If you don't get enough deep sleep during the night, you'll probably wake up feeling tired, as if you didn't sleep at all.

Deep sleep is also critical for growth. A chemical called **growth hormone,** which promotes the growth of body tissues, is produced in the brain by the **pituitary gland**. During deep sleep, the amount of growth hormone produced by the pituitary increases.

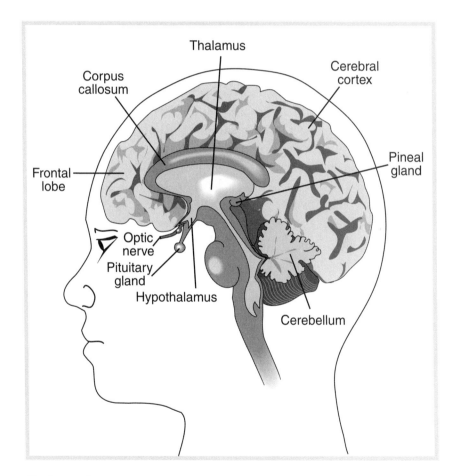

The human brain

The first nightly period of deep sleep can last from half an hour to more than an hour. At the end of the first deep-sleep period, your body suddenly moves, a signal that this stage of sleep is about to change. Within a few minutes, you move from Stage 4 sleep to a shallower stage, usually Stage 3, but sometimes Stage 2. Your body seems about to wake up, but it doesn't. Instead, you enter another type of sleep called **dream sleep**.

The Sleep that Dreams are Made Of

Stage 5 sleep, or dream sleep, is marked by jerky eye motions called **rapid eye movement (REM),** so dream sleep is also called **REM sleep.** (Sleep Stages 1 through 4 are typically called non-REM sleep.) If you watch the eyes of someone in REM sleep, you'll see their eyelids twitch. Beneath those twitching lids, their eyes are moving up and down. During REM sleep, heart rate and blood pressure increase, and the brain is busy creating dream after dream.

In a way, every dream you have is your own Hollywood movie, shown on an invisible screen on the back of your eyelids. In your dreams, you might be flying over the Grand Canyon, singing with a hot new band, or hitting the game-winning home run in the World Series. But all these sights and sounds come from your brain and are projected, in a way, on your eyelids. Your eyes flit around this screen, watching all the action.

Although your eyes are in constant motion during REM sleep, the rest of your body is motionless. When you are awake, nerve impulses from the brain pass through the spinal cord and on through the body, stimulating and controlling muscle movement. During REM sleep, however, those signals are blocked in the upper spinal cord. Without nerve impulses from the brain, your muscles do not move.

When REM sleep begins, blood flow to an area of the brain called the **thalamus** increases. Generally, increased blood flow to an area of the brain means that the area is more active than usual.

By monitoring, blood flow researchers can figure out which parts of the brain are regulating certain activities or processes. The thalamus is located deep inside the brain and close to the brain's sleep center. It acts as a kind of relay station, passing nerve signals between the brain and the spinal cord. A greater amount of blood flowing to the thalamus, and to another structure called the **amygdala,** during REM sleep may indicate that these areas play a part in creating dreams.

REM sleep doesn't last long. After 5 or 10 minutes, your body changes position and you begin to move through the stages of sleep again—to Stage 1 sleep for a minute or two, and then on to Stage 2, Stage 3, and finally, Stage 4 sleep. At the end of Stage 4, you'll enter REM sleep again. This cycle may be repeated four or five times each night.

Night Cycles

Each sleep cycle after the first one lasts about 90 minutes. Starting at about age 12, a person tends to spend about one-fourth of the night in REM sleep, one-fourth in deep sleep (Stages 3 and 4), and one-half in shallow sleep (Stage 2). The number of cycles you pass through each night depends partly on how long you sleep. The longer you sleep, the more cycles you pass through and the more dreams you'll have. The amount of time spent in each cycle also changes during the night. We spend a relatively greater amount of time in Stages 3 and 4 sleep at the beginning of the night and relatively more time in REM sleep toward the morning. Some researchers believe we can dream during any stage of sleep, but most experts agree that the most vivid dreams occur during REM sleep.

Most of us don't remember many of the dreams we have. Dreams are stored in an area of the brain that doesn't hold memories for long. But if you try to remember a dream right away, before your memory of the dream disappears, you'll probably be able to remember most or all of it. For instance, if you awaken from a dream with a start, you'll probably remember what you were dreaming about. If you awaken slowly, you probably won't be able to remember. Other thoughts will have passed through your mind as you were waking up and the delay is usually long enough for your dream to disappear from memory. After passing through four or five complete sleep cycles and watching dozens of dream-movies, you wake up—refreshed, alert, and ready to start the day.

Chapter 2

The Rhythm of Sleep

Y ou may sleep late on the weekends but you do, eventually, get up—even if nobody tries to wake you. And later that night, perhaps at the end of your favorite television show, you head off to bed and go to sleep.

What makes you wake up in the morning, even in a quiet house with nobody trying to wake you? Why don't you just sleep all morning and all afternoon? What causes you to feel drowsy at night and eventually drop off to sleep?

Believe it or not, the answer to both questions is—light.

You've Got Rhythm

Deep inside your brain lies a group of nerve cells called the **suprachiasmatic nucleus (SCN).** These cells act as a kind of clock that tells your body when to get up and when to go to sleep. The SCN resets itself each day, just as you might reset your alarm clock before you go to bed.

The resetting of the SCN depends on the regular appearance of light and the darkness that follows it. Without the light and dark

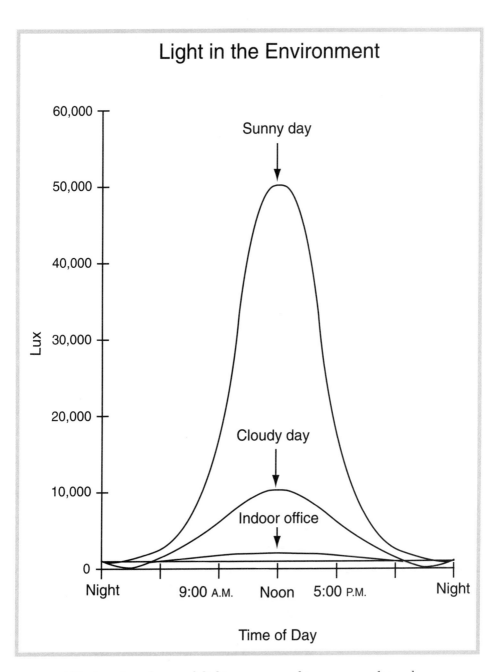

This chart shows how much light we are exposed to on a sunny day and a cloudy day. It also shows that people who spend the day inside are exposed to far less light.

cycle, the SCN can't figure out how to regulate the body's natural sleep-wake cycle.

The amount of light falling on Earth each day varies, depending on cloud cover and location. Indoor areas, of course, receive less light. The chart on the previous page shows how much light people are exposed to in **lux**, a measurement of the brightness of light.

Daily wake-up times and bedtimes are part of the body's natural sleep-wake cycle. This cycle is one of the body's several **circadian rhythms**—natural occurrences that have 24-hour cycles. Humans experience several circadian rhythms each day. For instance, growth hormone levels rise and fall in a particular pattern throughout the day. The level of this hormone reaches its peak shortly after you fall asleep, drops during the night, stays low all day long, and then rises again during sleep. Your body temperature also follows a natural cycle. It peaks between 10:00 A.M. and 2:00 P.M. and drops to a 24-hour low in the middle of the night, at around 3:00 A.M.

The sleep-wake cycle, one of the strongest circadian rhythms in the body, resets itself every day in response to light. A famous experiment carried out in 1938 showed the strong effect sunlight has on circadian rhythms. Two sleep researchers, Nathaniel Kleitman and Bruce Richardson, spent 33 days underground in Mammoth Cave, Kentucky. During that period, they completely lost track of time. The researchers woke when their body signaled them to wake, and fell asleep when they were sleepy. Soon, the researchers were falling asleep about an hour later than they would have if they had been exposed to the daily cycles of sunlight and darkness. At the end of the first week, the researchers were going to sleep about 7 hours later than they did at the start of the experiment.

The amount of daylight a person is exposed to varies by location. People living far from the equator—in Alaska, for example—may experience only a few hours of sunlight in the winter, a condition that can disrupt their circadian rhythms.

Two sleep researchers lived in Kentucky's Mammoth Cave for a month. Their studies helped scientists learn about the sleep-wake cycle.

The results of the Mammoth Cave experiment and other experiments like it, led researchers to believe that the body's sleep-wake cycle doesn't match the 24-hour clock by which we live our lives. They believed that natural cycle is actually 25 to 26 hours long. Because a person's natural sleep-wake cycle doesn't match the 24-hour clock, the researchers reasoned, it doesn't take much to disturb our ability to sleep at night.

Then, in early 1999, researchers in Boston determined that the body's natural sleep-wake cycle was actually 24 hours and 13 minutes, to be exact. Dr. Charles Czeisler of Brigham and Women's Hospital in Boston, Massachusetts, along with sleep researchers at Harvard University in Cambridge, Massachusetts, performed experiments similar to those done by sleep researchers in the past. The only difference was that these researchers more closely controlled the amount of artificial light to which the research subjects were exposed. The results indicated that the SCN is far more sensitive to light than was once thought.

The SCN receives signals from a chemical that is released from the eye when light shines on it. Light falling on the eye is made up of a wide range of colors, including reds, yellows, and blues. The light-absorbing chemical, called **cryptochrome,** absorbs blue light and transfers chemical signals to the **optic nerve,** the main nerve leading from the eye to the brain. The optic nerve carries the signals to the SCN.

The SCN, in turn, tells the nearby **pineal gland** to produce a sleep chemical called melatonin. Based on signals from the SCN, the pineal gland produces more melatonin or closes down production of the chemical.

Melatonin acts as a kind of sleep messenger. It travels through the body and tells cells to slow their activity. The pineal gland releases little melatonin during the day, when body cells are usually running full force. As the sun sets, however, the pineal gland begins pouring out melatonin, causing cell activities to gradually slow as the body prepares for sleep.

The body's melatonin level reaches its peak at around midnight.

Exposure to even small amounts of light in the late evening, when melatonin levels are high, can reduce the flow of melatonin until it reaches daytime levels. This decrease in melatonin can throw off the body's natural sleep-wake cycle. Teenagers are particularly affected by variations in melatonin levels.

During the early to mid-teen years, the pineal gland begins to release melatonin later in the evening than usual. As a result, teens are able to stay up later without feeling tired. Sleep often doesn't arrive until after midnight.

Because many high schools start classes earlier in the morning than at most elementary and junior high schools, teenagers may need to wake up before they've had enough sleep. A conflict begins between the alarm clock, which is telling the person to get up, and the teen's internal body clock that is demanding 2 more hours of sleep. It may take several hours for the body clock to catch up so that the teen feels alert and ready for the day's activities.

Some school districts in the United States have solved this problem by starting high school classes later. The later starting time allows teens to sleep and wake according to their natural rhythms and thus get the rest they need to do their best in school.

Resetting the Body Clock

Light is essential in resetting the body clock. Many blind people are highly affected by the absence of light and, as a result, they often experience sleep problems. Exposure to bright light in the morning can reset the body clock by as much as 90 minutes a day. That means that if you stay up 2 hours past your normal bedtime on Friday night, and 1 hour later on Saturday night, your body clock will end up being a total of 3 hours behind. Exposing yourself to bright light for two mornings in a row can reset your body clock back to where it belongs.

Your body clock can also act as a kind of internal alarm clock when you really need to wake up on time. Maybe you need to leave early for a bus trip to your school's championship game or to catch a plane. You're concerned that you might not wake up in time. You're afraid your alarm clock might fail. Or maybe you'll turn the alarm off in your sleep. In such instances, a chemical called **adrenocorticotropic hormone (ACTH),** helps set an internal alarm clock. Normally, ACTH and other chemicals help the body respond to stress or prepare for stressful events. For instance, when you're facing an important test but you haven't studied enough, the level of ACTH in your bloodstream shoots up. When the stressful event has passed, the ACTH level drops back to normal.

Researchers at the University of Texas Medical Branch in Galveston found that ACTH levels rise during sleep just as they do during the day. The researchers monitored ACTH levels in 15 volunteers at various times during the night and early morning. The tests showed that when the volunteers planned to wake up at a certain time, ACTH levels shot up quickly about an hour or so before the wake-up time. When the volunteers had no plans to wake up early, their ACTH levels rose much more slowly. It's as though the brain has its own alarm clock and, well before the real alarm clock buzzes, the brain tells the body to pour out the ACTH.

Larks and Owls

No matter what kind of clock you use to wake up—internal or external—you are probably most alert in either the morning or the evening. If you're more alert in the morning, you're a morning person. Sleep researchers would call you a lark, after the meadowlark, a bird that sings at sunrise.

On the other hand, if you're most alert in the evening and you enjoy staying up late at night, you're a night person. Sleep

*Like this Everglades barred owl
(left), human "owls" tend to feel
more alert at night.
Like this meadowlark (right),
human "larks" tend to feel
energized in the morning and
sluggish at night.*

researchers would call you an owl, after the bird that is active at night.

Most people have characteristics of both larks and owls. One of the key differences between larks and owls is in their body temperature variation. Body temperature normally varies by up to 1 degree Celsius over a 24-hour period. Peak alertness levels usually occur when body temperature is highest. A lark's body temperature tends to rise quickly in the morning and stay relatively steady until the early evening. As the evening wears on, the lark's body temperature drops. Soon, drowsiness sets in and the person feels ready for bed.

An owl's body temperature rises more slowly in the morning and reaches a peak in the evening. Then, in the late evening, the owl's body temperature finally begins to fall.

Whether you're a lark or a night owl depends almost entirely on the genetic traits your parents passed on to you. In other words, once a lark, always a lark, and once an owl, always an owl.

Knowing the time of day when you are most alert can help you adjust your lifestyle to fit the pattern. If you know you're a lark, you might want to study for a test in the afternoon rather than in the evening. If you're a night owl, you might want to study in the evening rather than in the morning or afternoon.

Chapter 3

Sleep Deprivation

R andy Gardner chose an interesting research project for his high school science fair. In 1965, when Randy was 17 years old, he decided to try to get into the *Guinness Book of World Records* by staying awake longer than anyone on record. To break the previous record, he would have to keep his eyes open for more than 11 days.

In the beginning, he played cards with friends, exercised, took cold showers, and walked around—anything to keep himself awake. After 2 days, he was exhausted. He couldn't focus his eyes enough to read or watch television, and his eyelids were so heavy that he couldn't keep them open. Randy walked around with his head tilted back so that he could see.

After 3 days without sleep, Randy become irritable and quick to anger. He told his friends to leave him alone. After 4 days, he began seeing things that weren't there—fog around street lamps, a tweed suit made of worms, and other bizarre visions.

After 9 days without sleep, Randy was unable to speak in full sentences. He couldn't remember things that had happened just moments before. Was he ready to give in and go to sleep? Not a chance! He was determined to beat the record.

On the eleventh night, he played basketball at an arcade with one of the most famous sleep researchers in the world—William Dement of Stanford University, in Stanford, California. Randy played 100 games against the well-rested researcher and won them all!

Randy broke the world's record the next day by logging 264 consecutive hours—11 full days and nights—without sleep. That night, he slept just under 15 hours. The next night he slept only 8 hours. Randy was soon sleeping his pre-record standard of about 7 hours a night.

Dangerous Deprivation

Few other people have experienced the kind of **sleep deprivation,** or lack of sleep, that Randy volunteered for. Luckily, Randy didn't drive while he was going after the record. If he had, he almost certainly would have had an accident.

The National Highway Traffic Safety Administration (NHTSA) says that sleep deprivation leads to as many as 100,000 accidents in the United States each year. According to the NHTSA, a typical accident caused by a sleep-deprived person involves a single vehicle driving off the road. These accidents generally occur at night, often on highways in rural areas with little traffic.

The *Exxon Valdez* oil spill was one of the most infamous sleep-related accidents of the past century. In 1989, as the huge oil tanker made its way through Prince William Sound in Alaska, the sleep-deprived third mate took the helm. Not long after the third mate took over, the tanker struck a reef. About 11 million gallons (42 million liters) of oil poured into the water, making the *Exxon Valdez* spill the worst in U.S. history.

A nearly catastrophic accident at Three Mile Island nuclear

The ship the Exxon Valdez *surrounded by oil spilled from its hull. Sleep deprivation is blamed for the accident.*

power plant (located near Harrisburg, Pennsylvania) was also related to sleep deprivation. In 1979, a sleep-impaired worker at the plant didn't realize that highly radioactive material was leaking out of a storage tank. Although the material never escaped into the environment, the worker's error could easily have led to the release of large amounts of radioactive debris. The accident resulted in the evacuation of thousands of people.

A similar accident occurred at Chernobyl nuclear power plant in Ukraine, then part of the Soviet Union. In the early morning hours of April 26, 1986, sleep-deprived engineers failed to take the proper precautions during an experiment. The subsequent explosion released an enormous cloud of radioactive gas into the atmosphere. Radioactive gas drifted for thousands of miles, and was even detected in parts of western Europe. Dozens of people and animals living near the plant died, and more than 100,000 people were evacuated from their homes. Most never returned.

Many sleep-related motor-vehicle accidents occur because the driver experiences what is known as **microsleep.** During microsleep, a person fights to stay awake, but suddenly falls into a brief period of Stage I sleep, the lightest level of sleep. Brain waves recorded before and during microsleep show rapid bursts of electrical activity. It's as if the brain is trying to jerk itself awake, but can't.

Microsleep usually lasts just 1 or 2 seconds but can last as long as 30 seconds. During that time, the person remains standing or sitting up but his or her mind takes a kind of mini-vacation. Microsleeps occur most often when the individual is doing something boring or repetitive, such as working on an assembly line or driving along a deserted highway.

According to a 1999 study, lack of sleep leads to the same level of slowed reflexes and unclear thinking that is caused by alcohol. In fact, the reflexes of a sleep-deprived person are as slow and uncoordinated as those of someone who is legally drunk. With slower reflexes, a person cannot react quickly in an emergency.

Effects of Sleep Deprivation

On a day-to-day basis, losing an hour or two of sleep can lead to daytime sleepiness, moodiness, irritability, and poor performance—on the job or in school. A sleep-deprived person might feel sad or angry more readily and might not be able to handle problems as easily as when rested. The person's memory might fail and the person's hands may shake. The eyelids may twitch from fatigue. Other effects of sleep loss include greater sensitivity to pain and an increased appetite.

The loss of a full night's sleep can cause extreme daytime sleepiness and a disruption of sleep the next night. Failing to get enough sleep night after night creates a **sleep debt,** in which the

Scientists estimate that half of all Americans are regularly sleep deprived.

effects of sleep deprivation build up over time. If you've ever suffered a sleep debt, you know that you lose interest in the things around you. You make more mistakes than you normally would and you have trouble judging distance or depth. "In the simplest terms," sleep researcher William Dement said, "a large sleep debt makes you stupid."

A person who goes through life with a significant sleep debt may also regularly experience headaches, stomach irritation, and various intestinal problems. Researchers estimate that about half of the adults in the United States don't get as much sleep as they need. As James Maas, a sleep expert and psychologist at Cornell University in New York City said, "We've become a nation of walking zombies."

How Much Sleep Is Enough?

The amount of sleep we need varies with age. Newborns need about 16 to 20 hours of sleep each day. They sleep as much during the day as during the night. When the baby is about 6 months old, his or her sleeping pattern changes. By this time, the typical baby is sleeping through the night and takes one or two short naps during the day. As children age, they tend not to require as much sleep. In general, toddlers need 12 to 14 hours and preschoolers need about 12 hours of sleep every 24 hours. Kids aged 6 to 9 years need about 10 hours, while 10- to 12-year olds need slightly less sleep, generally between 9 and 11 hours. Teenagers need an average of 9 hours and 15 minutes of sleep each night but typically get much less—an average of about 6 1/2 hours. That means most teenagers go about their daily lives sleep-deprived. Mary Carskadon, a leading sleep researcher at Brown University in Providence, Rhode Island, has been studying sleep deprivation among teens for several years. In one experiment, Dr. Carskadon asked her students to take naps during the day and then studied their brain waves and other vital signs as they slept. She found that many teens passed into dream sleep, or REM

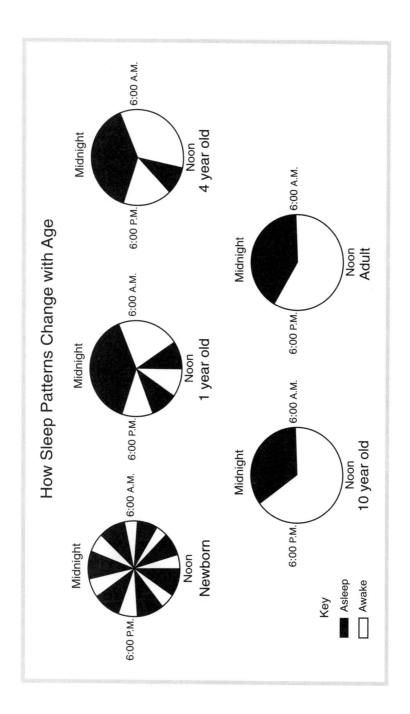

How Sleep Patterns Change with Age

Newborn

1 year old

4 year old

10 year old

Adult

Key
Asleep
Awake

Midnight
Noon
6:00 A.M.
6:00 P.M.

41

sleep, within just four minutes. A healthy adult who gets a good night's sleep might take about 2 hours to reach REM sleep. The teens' remarkably rapid dip into REM sleep is a sign of significant sleep deprivation.

According to Dr. Carskadon, the brain of a typical teenager isn't ready to wake up until around 9:00 A.M. "Their brains are telling them it's nighttime," Dr. Carskadon said, "and the rest of the world is saying it's time to go to school." Those last couple of hours of sleep in the morning—sleep many teens don't get—can be critical for memory and learning. The longest period of REM sleep tends to occur in the early morning hours. Teens whose alarm clocks waken them after only 5 or 6 hours of sleep do not complete that last period of REM sleep. A lack of REM sleep can lead to impaired memory, poor judgment, irritability, and depression. Studies indicate that teens who don't get enough sleep tend to earn C's and D's in school, while those who get plenty of sleep tend to earn As and Bs.

Although the total amount of sleep needed by an adult stays about the same throughout life, the pattern of that sleep changes over time.

How Work Patterns Affect Sleep

Many shift workers start their shift at 3 or 4 o'clock in the after-noon and work until 11 or 12 o'clock at night. Others work the night shift, which usually starts at 11 or 12 o'clock and finishes at 7 or 8 o'clock in the morning. Teens who go to school during the day and then work in the evening, only to go home and do home-work until 11 or 12 o'clock, have many of the problems faced by people who do shift work.

About 20 percent of the people in the United States are involved in shift work or are **on call.** Being on call means that you can be called to work at any hour. Doctors, nurses, volunteer firefighters, plumbers and electric-company repair personnel may all be on call.

42

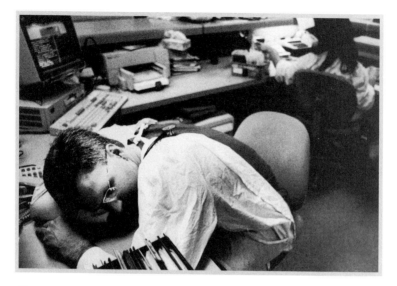

This emergency room physician has fallen asleep on the job. It's not easy working the night shift.

Many people who are on-call or do shift work are often awake at night and asleep—or at least trying to sleep—during the day. Even under the best conditions, daytime sleep tends to last about 2 hours less than nighttime sleep, partly as a result of normal variations in body temperature. The body tends to be most alert when body temperature increases and least alert when body temperature drops. Body temperature climbs throughout the day and peaks in the evening. It then drops during the night, reaching its lowest point in the early morning hours.

These variations in body temperature mean that a person with a daytime job is heading to bed as his body temperature—and level of alertness—drops. By contrast, a person with a nighttime job is trying to sleep during the day, when body temperature is increasing and the level of alertness is rising. No wonder it can be so hard to sleep during the day!

In addition to body-temperature variations, typical daytime

noises can make it more difficult to fall asleep. The sounds of traffic, voices, or aircraft flying overhead are more likely to prevent a person from sleeping during the day than at night. Even a small amount of sunlight seeping into a bedroom can be enough to prevent the body clock from resetting itself. Together, the presence of sunlight, noise, and a rising body temperature combine to make daytime sleeping extremely difficult.

Worse yet are the effects of **rotating shifts.** Some people work the day shift for a while—perhaps a week or two—and then rotate to the evening or night shift. After a while, they rotate to another shift and eventually back to the day shift. As a result, they're constantly trying to adjust their sleep-wake patterns to fit their work schedule.

For instance, if a person who is accustomed to sleeping at night is rotated to the night shift, he or she must suddenly change gears and try to sleep during the day. Then, just as the worker gets accustomed to sleeping during the day, the schedule changes and the worker's sleep pattern must be adjusted all over again.

Studies indicate that if a day-shift worker is able to adjust the sleep-wake cycle 90 minutes per day, it takes a week for the body clock to fully adjust to night-shift work. By that time, the worker is often rotated to another shift, and the pattern starts all over again.

And that's just for a Monday-through-Friday work schedule. Many shift workers must then adjust their sleep schedules for the weekend, so that they can be with their family during "normal" hours. The worker doesn't want to be asleep while a son plays in his first basketball game or a daughter plays in her soccer championship.

Continual adjustments in the sleep-wake cycle can lead to long-term sleep deprivation. Studies indicate that shift workers are generally more tired, more irritable, and less able to concentrate than people who are not involved in shift work. They also tend to be **obese,** or extremely overweight, in poor physical condition, and prone to stomach problems, particularly ulcers.

In addition, shift workers may drink large amounts of coffee in an effort to stay awake at work. Caffeine effects are long-lasting, however, and may interfere with the ability to fall asleep later. Also, workers may begin to drink alcohol regularly to help them fall asleep. Rather than helping the person sleep, however, alcohol actually interferes with sleep. It reduces the amount of time spent in REM sleep and causes the individual to wake up earlier and more often than normal.

People involved in on-call work tend to have slightly different problems. Although they usually sleep during nighttime hours, they know they might be awakened at any moment. Under these conditions, sleep tends to be lighter, with shorter periods of deep sleep. And deep sleep is the period of sleep that supplies the body with the most beneficial rest.

If the person is called into work, he or she may miss entire periods of deep sleep and perhaps several periods of REM sleep too. Lack of deep sleep and REM sleep can lead to daytime drowsiness, irritability, and other effects of sleep deprivation.

Sleeping on a Jet Plane

Have you ever traveled a long distance by plane? Do any of the adults in your house frequently travel by plane? If so, you or your parent might have experienced jet lag, a disruption in the body's sleep-wake cycle as a result of traveling across several time zones in a jet airplane.

The world has 24 time zones—regions divided along imaginary north-to-south lines. In general, time in one zone is exactly one hour different than time in the zones on each side. For instance, if it's 9:00 A.M. in Chicago (located in a time zone called Central Standard Time), then it's 10:00 A.M. in the time zone to the east (Eastern Standard Time) and 8:00 A.M. in the time zone to the west (Mountain Standard Time).

The more time zones crossed, the greater the effects of jet

Flying across times zones has thrown off this woman's sleep-wake cycle. She is taking a short nap between flights.

lag. People who fly across several time zones may spend an entire day in the air and end up having that time added to—or subtracted from—their day. For instance, a flight leaving New York, New York at 8:00 A.M. may take 6 hours to reach Los Angeles, California. If time in Los Angeles were measured according to Eastern Standard Time (EST), travelers would step off the plane in Los Angeles at 2:00 P.M. But because Los Angeles is three hours behind New York, clocks there would actually read 11:00 A.M. The traveler would gain 3 hours that day. Depending on how many time zones you cross, it may take several days for your body clock to adjust to the new sleep-wake cycle.

Generally, your body clock adjusts more easily to longer days than it does to shorter days. As a result, travelers who fly eastward (Los Angeles to New York, for instance) tend to experience less severe jet lag than people who fly westward (from New York to Los Angeles, for instance).

Chapter 4

Sleep Disorders

Both adults and teenagers may experience sleep disorders. Many people have insomnia—difficulty in falling asleep or in staying asleep. Other common sleep disorders are sleepwalking, snoring, and teeth grinding. Less common disorders include night terrors, obstructive sleep apnea, restless leg syndrome, and a rare condition called narcolepsy.

Insomnia

It's 11:00 P.M. and you've been in bed for half an hour, but you just can't fall asleep. You get a snack and head back to bed, hoping you'll be able to nod off. At 12:05 A.M. you still can't sleep. *This is ridiculous,* you say to yourself. *I've got to get some sleep. Why can't I sleep?* At 12:55 A.M., you're still awake—tossing, turning, and hoping sleep comes soon.

Has this ever happened to you? Have you had nights when you just couldn't sleep, no matter how hard you tried? If so, you've experienced insomnia. People with insomnia may have trouble falling asleep or be unable to fall back to sleep. Some people with insomnia fall asleep easily but wake up too early in the morning. Other people with insomnia just don't sleep well. After only one night with insomnia, you may feel tired all day and lack the energy to complete even routine tasks. You may have trouble concentrating and feel irritable.

Temporary insomnia can be brought on by stress, trying to sleep in a noisy place, or one that's too hot or too cold, or sleeping in an unfamiliar place. Some drugs, such as cold remedies and diet pills, may also cause insomnia. Even falling in love—that great feeling you get when you meet someone really special— can cause sleepless nights.

Longer-lasting insomnia can result from depression, medical conditions that can disrupt sleep such as arthritis (a joint disease), kidney disease, heart failure, or asthma—a breathing disorder. Insomnia can strike people of any age, but it tends to occur more often among people over 60 and people suffering from depression. Insomnia is often the result of a combination of factors. Poor sleeping habits and stress can make insomnia worse.

Most of the time, insomnia is mild and clears up by itself. But sometimes insomnia lasts weeks or months. In such cases, a person can get into a pattern of sleeplessness. If you believe you are not going to sleep, your body begins to "believe" you. It basically "learns" not to fall asleep. The more often you experience insomnia, the better your body becomes at not sleeping.

If you find yourself unable to sleep at night, start getting up at the same time every morning, Do this for two weeks, including weekends. Make sure you expose yourself to sunlight or other bright light as soon as you get up. Sunlight is essential in resetting the body clock. If possible, stay exposed to the light for at least an hour.

Most people with mild insomnia can reset their body clock this way and put themselves back on schedule within about 2 weeks. Soon they're falling asleep just minutes after they close their eyes at night. For more stubborn cases of insomnia, a doctor might recommend over-the-counter sleeping aids or a prescription sleep aid.

A type of therapy called **stimulus control** can also help relieve insomnia. In this type of therapy, a person avoids doing things that signal wakefulness rather than sleepiness. For example, many people with insomnia try to sleep in all sorts of places other than the bedroom because they can't sleep in bed. They may sleep on the couch, in a chair, on the floor, or even in the car. At the same time, they may use their bed for studying, talking on the phone, or other activities besides sleep.

If you're having trouble sleeping at night, avoid using your bed for activities other than sleeping.

In stimulus control, a person uses the bed *only* for sleeping, not for studying or chatting on the phone. The person also makes sure that he tries to sleep *only* in bed, not in other places. People who can't sleep are supposed to get out of bed. Eventually, a person associates being in bed with sleeping.

Walking in Your Sleep

Nick was 11 years old when he walked into a corner of his family's living room and started to pull down his pajama bottoms as if he were getting ready to urinate. His astonished mother gently turned him around and guided him to the toilet in the bathroom. The next morning, when Nick's mother told him what he had done the night before, he giggled, blushed, and said he had no memory of the incident.

Nick was sleepwalking. In a typical episode, the sleepwalker gets out of bed in a daze, shuffles around the room, mumbles something, and then returns to bed. The sleepwalker may appear dazed but moves around as if there's a definite purpose for being out of bed.

If you ask, "What's the matter?" or "Where are you going?" you may get an answer that seems to make sense—but really doesn't. The next morning, the sleepwalker remembers little, if anything, about the episode.

Although few adults sleepwalk, many children do it at least once in their lives. About 1 in 10 children sleepwalks repeatedly. Sleepwalking can happen anytime after a child learns to walk, though it tends to occur most often between the ages of 4 and 12. Children are more likely to sleepwalk if their parents sleepwalked when they were children.

Among children, sleepwalking is considered a normal behavior that rarely causes problems. Sleepwalking in adults can result from heavy alcohol use, severe fatigue, or excessive physical activity during the day. Alcohol, fatigue, and exertion tend to cause a person to spend more time in deep sleep, which in turn increases the chance of sleepwalking.

People who sleepwalk don't just walk around their bed. They may leave the room or even walk out of their home. Sleepwalkers can hurt themselves. Some people have fallen off balconies, down stairs, or into swimming pools.

Sleepwalking usually occurs during the period between deep sleep and a lighter level of sleep. It's most likely to occur during the first three hours of the night. In an episode of sleepwalking, it's as if the body wakes up but the mind doesn't, preferring the comfort of deep, nondreaming sleep. Little wonder, then, that the sleepwalker seems confused. The person's body can't figure out whether it's awake or asleep! Most children who sleepwalk require no treatment. The condition probably won't last long and as long as the child is in familiar surroundings it shouldn't cause problems. A person who tends to sleepwalk should avoid exercising, eating a heavy meal, or drinking fluids containing caffeine or alcohol close to bedtime. And follow the same routines each night. Changing the routine can sometimes bring on a sleepwalking episode.

If someone in your family sleepwalks, try not to startle the sleepwalker if you catch them in the act, and don't try to wake him or her. Speak softly and, with a light touch, gently guide the person back to bed. Encourage the sleepwalker to get plenty of rest throughout the week because the condition is more likely to occur when the person is tired.

Although sleepwalking episodes are rare, they can present safety problems. A sleepwalker who sleeps in a bunk bed should be assigned to the bottom bunk. The doors leading outside should be locked. Take any sharp objects out of the bedroom. Keep the sleepwalker away from swimming pools and other unsafe areas. Ask an adult to make sure all firearms and other weapons are locked safely away to avoid accidents. Finally, hallways should be well lit to prevent falls.

Snoring

Remember Bert and Ernie, the Sesame Street characters? Remember how they both snored? Bert would start it off with an ear-splitting *snrrfffffffff*, and then Ernie would finish it off with a high-pitched whistle. Snoring might be cute when Bert and Ernie do it, but it isn't so cute when you're in a room with someone who snores. A loud, regular snore can prevent you from getting a good night's sleep. If it is any comfort to you, the person who is snoring may not be getting a good night's sleep either.

Snoring occurs when air no longer flows easily through the airways of the mouth and throat. The muscles in the throat that keep these airways open during the day tend to relax as we enter deep sleep. The jaw muscles become slack, the **uvula**—that little flap of tissue at the back of the throat—softens, and the tongue slides backward in the throat.

Sometimes the relaxed tongue, the softened muscles, and other tissues can block airflow. This blockage causes the soft tissues to vibrate, which causes snoring. The greater the vibration, the louder the snore.

Snoring usually occurs during deep sleep but may also occur during dream sleep. Snoring is more likely when people sleep on their back because the tongue is more likely to fall backward in the throat and block the flow of air.

About one in five adults snores on a regular basis. Men are more likely than women to snore, and older people are more likely to snore than younger people are. Snoring also tends to run in families and happens more often among overweight people. Their throat tissues tend to be thicker, which makes the air passage narrower.

Under certain conditions, average-sized individuals may also snore. Alcohol causes body tissues, including those in the throat, to relax, and that can lead to snoring. Sleeping pills, cold remedies, and numerous other drugs can also cause snoring, as can nasal congestion—a swelling of the tissues in the nose.

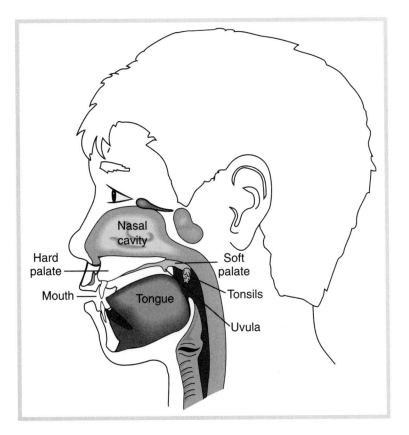

Structures of the mouth and throat

Enlarged **tonsils** are a common cause of snoring. The tonsils are clumps of infection-fighting tissue on each side of the throat. When a person has a cold or throat infection, his or her tonsils may swell, reducing the flow of air through the mouth.

If you snore, try sleeping on your side. This helps prevent your tongue from falling backward in your throat and causing you to snore. If you have a hard time sleeping on your side, try sewing a tennis ball into a pocket on the back of your pajamas. That will help keep you on your side! You might also raise the head of the bed to help open the airway between your mouth and lungs.

Try to get enough sleep every day. If you're overtired, you spend more time in deep sleep and that's when you are most likely to snore.

In severe cases, doctors can trim excess tissues from a person's mouth and throat. **Laser-assisted uvulopalatoplasty (LAUP)** is a 10-minute procedure in which a laser is used to cut away part of the uvula, the tonsils (if enlarged), and the **soft palate.** Doctors say LAUP reduces snoring in about 85 percent of snorers.

Night Terrors

Imagine you're baby-sitting your neighbor's 4-year-old son, Justin. You like Justin; it's easy to make him laugh, and he doesn't put up a fight when it's time for bed. One night, though, about an hour after you put him to bed, you hear a blood-curdling scream.

You rush to Justin's bedroom, afraid that he has fallen out of bed. When you get there, you find Justin thrashing around in bed and screaming as if he's terrified. You try to calm him down, but he continues to scream. You end up just watching him to make sure he doesn't hurt himself. Suddenly, Justin stops screaming and falls back to sleep. You've just witnessed an episode of night terror.

Night terrors are sudden, dramatic awakenings from deep sleep that happen in about 3 in 100 children. Night terrors typically occur in three- to five-year-olds, but they can also happen in older and younger children.

Most kids outgrow night terrors by first grade. If a parent had night terrors as a child, their child is more likely to have night terrors. A child is more likely to have night terrors if a brother, sister, or parent was—or *is*—a sleepwalker. Stress or fatigue can bring on night terrors.

A night terror is *not* a nightmare. Nightmares generally occur during dream sleep. After awakening from a nightmare, people are usually fully awake and can remember the nightmare. Night terrors are likely to occur within 2 hours of falling asleep, at the end of the first period of deep sleep. In a typical night-terror episode, a child suddenly sits upright in bed. His or her face is flushed and dripping with sweat. The child may appear awake but his or her brain is only partially alert. It is difficult to wake the child and he or she generally doesn't respond to anything you say.

A night terror episode typically lasts only a few minutes, though some can last as long as an hour. In the morning, children generally have no memory of the absolute terror they seemed to experience during the night.

When you are with someone who is having a night terror, try to stay calm. Night terrors do not indicate a health or psychological problem. They usually happen because children spend considerably more time in deep sleep than older children and adults. Well-rested kids tend to have fewer night-terror attacks than kids who feel tired all the time. Some doctors recommend that a child who has night terrors be awakened about half an hour before the time night terrors usually strike. The person should be kept awake for about 5 minutes, and then allowed to go back to sleep. Using this simple technique, called scheduled awakening, for several weeks can help prevent most episodes of night terrors.

Teeth Grinding

Did you ever wake up with aching jaws? Has anyone ever told you that they couldn't sleep because you were grinding your teeth so loudly? These are signs of **bruxism,** the medical term for teeth grinding.

Bruxism occurs in one out of four children. The condition can also occur in adults but it is more common in children. In bruxism, the sleeper's jaw muscles repeatedly tighten, or contract. That contraction causes the teeth to grind together, which creates a loud, grating sound that can send shivers down the spine of anyone who happens to be nearby. Sleepers don't hear their own teeth grinding, of course.

The forcefulness of the contraction can be so strong that it causes headaches and pain in front of the ear where the lower jaw meets the skull. It can also cause tooth pain (by wearing down the tooth enamel), or pain in the face, ear, or neck. In severe cases, bruxism can lead to swelling of the jaw or thinning of the jawbone.

Most episodes of teeth grinding last only a few seconds, and usually occur most often during Stage 2 or Stage 3 sleep. Teeth grinding can also occur during deep sleep or dream sleep, when the body is otherwise motionless.

Bruxism is more likely to occur in children when other family members grind their teeth at night. Certain jaw problems can also lead to teeth grinding, as can alcohol use. But stress is the most common cause of this condition. Anything that causes stress—an upcoming test, an argument with a friend, or not finishing your homework—can cause you to grind your teeth at night. In a way, you're chewing through your problems as you sleep.

Most experts agree that bruxism isn't necessarily a major health problem. Most people who grind their teeth are perfectly healthy. But if you grind your teeth, it's a good idea to visit your dentist to make sure you don't have jaw or tooth problems. If you have severe bruxism, you might need to wear a tooth guard. The guard is usually made of rubber or soft plastic. It doesn't stop the grinding, but it protects your teeth from being worn down. Learning how to deal with stress more effectively might also help you control bruxism and sleep better.

Obstructive Sleep Apnea

Watching a person with **obstructive sleep apnea** can be scary. In sleep apnea, an individual momentarily stops breathing. After a few initial deep breaths, breathing becomes more and more shallow until finally, another breath doesn't come. After 10 seconds or more, the sleeper takes a deep breath, often snoring at the same time. Regular breathing then resumes. The breaths gradually become shallow once again and the cycle repeats itself. Periods of apnea occur over and over again, usually during deep sleep. In some patients, apnea can occur hundreds of times a night.

The most common cause of obstructive sleep apnea is also the cause of snoring—extreme relaxation of tissues in the mouth and throat. When the tissues relax so much that they block or obstruct airflow completely, breathing stops.

At the start of a period of apnea, the oxygen level in the bloodstream begins to drop. The brain senses the drop in oxygen and sends a signal to the lungs to start breathing again. These signals may not work at first and so the person remains breathless. His or her shoulders may jerk, and his or her chest may jump in spasms. Eventually, the signals from the brain get through and the person breathes again.

Obstructive sleep apnea is most common in overweight men. The condition also occurs in children and teenagers. It is especially common in overweight teens who have other family members with the problem. Obstructive sleep apnea can also be caused by inflamed tonsils, which can restrict airflow.

Repeated periods of apnea can prevent a person from entering or staying in deep sleep. Each time the person stops breathing, the brain signals the lungs to breathe again, and that prevents the brain from entering the deeper levels of sleep. With hundreds of periods of apnea in a single night, a person with sleep apnea may get almost no sleep.

Without enough deep sleep, the body can't get the rest it needs. The person feels tired during the day and may experience dry mouth, irritability, and difficulty concentrating. Driving can be particularly dangerous for people with sleep apnea. In extreme cases, sleep apnea can lead to high blood pressure, heart attack, stroke, and dangerous heart rhythms.

Losing weight is the main treatment for sleep apnea. Weight

loss reduces the size of the tissues in the throat so that airflow isn't obstructed. People with sleep apnea should avoid alcohol and other drugs that can cause sleepiness. They should also avoid becoming overtired during the day. The more tired a person is at night, the more relaxed his throat tissues become during deep sleep and the greater the risk of sleep apnea. Removing enlarged tonsils usually cures sleep apnea in children and teens.

For people who don't respond to weight loss and other standard treatments, doctors may use **continuous positive airway pressure (CPAP)** (pronounced SEE-pap). In CPAP, a tight-fitting mask is worn over the nose during sleep. A tube attached to the mask supplies a constant flow of oxygen under slight pressure.

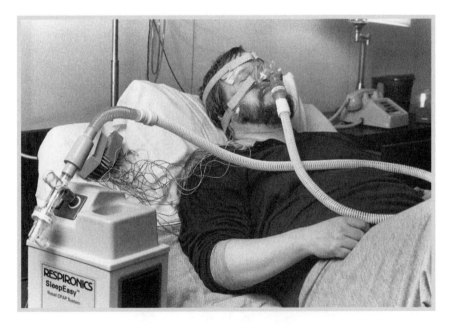

This man is being monitored at a sleep center. He is wearing a CPAP mask attached to a breathing machine. The mask and machine help keep the man's airway open during sleep and reduce the severity of sleep apnea.

The oxygen flow maintains constant air pressure in the throat which keeps the airways open. The person is less tired during the day and generally sleeps better at night.

When CPAP doesn't work, removal of excess tissues in the throat may be the only solution. Removal of excess tissues helps open the airway in the throat and prevents the airway from becoming blocked.

Many sleep experts use lasers to remove excess throat tissues. Others use a kind of radiowave to remove the tissue. This 10-minute procedure, called **somnoplasty,** is less painful and causes less bleeding than other forms of treatment.

Restless Leg Syndrome

Restless leg syndrome, (RLS) is a sleep disorder in which discomfort in the legs causes a person to jerk them. People with RLS describe the feeling as an irritation, a tingling sensation in the legs, or an ache deep in the bones. All these sensations are accompanied by an overwhelming urge to move. **Periodic limb movement disorder (PLMD)** is a related but separate disorder. In some cases, the two disorders occur together. PLMD occurs mainly in older adults, but may start in childhood. PLMD is characterized by repetitive, forceful limb movements—usually kicking. Often the person doing the kicking isn't aware of it.

As many as 12 million people in the United States suffer from RLS. The disorder is most common among older adults and pregnant women, but may afflict children and teens as well. Episodes of RLS usually strike during the early stages of sleep. The condition occurs more often after someone has done hard, physical work or had caffeine. Stress and fatigue can also trigger RLS.

Doctors aren't sure what causes RLS. One theory suggests that as the muscles begin to relax during the first stage of sleep, something goes wrong. The muscles overreact to even the slightest stimulation, such as the touch of the sheet. That overreaction may lead to the pain or tingling that often occurs with RLS. A lack of vitamin B_{12} or the mineral calcium may also play a role.

To reduce the number of episodes of RLS, doctors may give their patients vitamin supplements with calcium. A drug called talipexole is one of several prescription medicines that can reduce episodes of RLS. A person with RLS should avoid caffeine in any form, liquid (coffee, tea, or cola) or solid (chocolate). Leg massage, stretching exercises, and exercises designed to build endurance may also help prevent attacks of RLS.

Narcolepsy

George is a good student. He studies hard and gets good grades. There's just one problem: he falls asleep all the time. One minute, George will be performing a science experiment with some classmates. The next minute, his head drops onto the lab bench with a thud and he's sound asleep. A few seconds later, George wakes up and tries to continue what he had been doing before the attack.

It's not that George is sleepy all the time; he has narcolepsy, a sleep disorder that causes someone to fall asleep at a time when he should be fully awake. An attack of narcolepsy can last from just a few seconds to 30 minutes or more. Thousands of people in the United States suffer from narcolepsy. They fall asleep in school, on the field or court, or even while talking on the phone. One of every 1,000 people in the United States suffers from narcolepsy. The first signs of the disorder usually appear during the teen years or in early adulthood, but may appear as early as age 10. In a teenager with narcolepsy, the disorder may first appear as excessive sleepiness. Some teens with narcolepsy are wrongly called lazy or disinterested.

The excessive sleepiness of narcolepsy can't be explained by logical reasons such as staying up late the night before or a lack of sleep. If a teen always gets a good night's sleep, isn't depressed, doesn't have a medical condition, and isn't taking drugs that would cause the sleepiness, narcolepsy should be suspected.

Many people with narcolepsy also experience **cataplexy,** a condition in which muscles suddenly become paralyzed. Cataplexy typically occurs during a period of excitement or other intense emotion. One woman fell asleep while playing cards with her friends. Her head dropped on the table in the middle of a hand.

The exact cause of narcolepsy is not known. Some scientists think a disruption in certain brain chemicals may be the cause. Recent evidence suggests that the tendency to develop narcolepsy passes from one generation to the next. This tendency seems particularly noticeable among people of Japanese descent. In Japan, one of three people has narcolepsy—the highest known rate of narcolepsy in the world.

Regardless of the cause, people with narcolepsy experience sleep in a totally different way than other people. Most people pass through several non-REM sleep stages before entering REM sleep, the sleep of dreams. However, an individual with narcolepsy passes directly into REM sleep, bypassing non-REM sleep. It's as if the narcoleptic individual passes from the "real world" to a world of dreams in just a second or two.

Narcolepsy can't be cured, but it can be treated with drugs that help keep the person awake during the day. The drug methylphenidate (Ritalin) has been used to stimulate nerves in the brain and spinal cord and prevent daytime sleepiness. Modafinil (Provigil) was approved for treating narcolepsy in 1999. This drug causes fewer side effects than other drugs and may prove helpful for many patients with narcolepsy.

For patients with cataplexy and narcolepsy, many doctors use drugs that help balance important brain chemicals. The drugs, commonly used to treat depression, help prevent the sudden muscle weakness that occurs in cataplexy.

Sleeping pills may be used to help narcoleptics sleep at night.

Because sleep is altered in narcolepsy, many people with the disorder have difficulty getting enough deep sleep at night. The lack of deep sleep adds to the severity of daytime sleepiness.

Herbal medicines and acupuncture may provide relief for some individuals. Experts also offer a number of lifestyle tips for people with narcolepsy. First, it's important that the person with narcolepsy maintains a regular sleep-wake schedule. Going to bed at the same time every night and getting up at the same time every morning can be critical for getting enough deep sleep at night.

The narcoleptic should also take regular, short daytime naps. People with narcolepsy are generally most alert after a nap. Scheduling a nap at certain times during the day can help limit

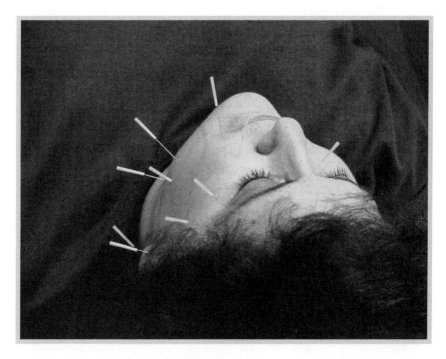

Acupuncture may help reduce daytime sleepiness in people with narcolepsy.

daytime sleepiness. Avoiding boring or repetitive tasks during periods of low alertness can also help prevent sudden attacks of sleep. Avoiding alcohol and other drugs may also help.

Caffeine may help increase alertness during the day, but it should be avoided at night because it can prevent a person from sleeping. Narcoleptics should avoid dangerous activities, particularly when they also experience cataplexy. Driving, swimming, operating machinery, and caring for an infant can all pose grave risks for narcoleptics. They must be constantly aware of the possibility of falling asleep suddenly and take precautions to prevent harm to themselves or others.

Chapter 5

Toward a More Restful Sleep

If you're one of the millions of people who experience regular sleep problems, particularly insomnia, you can do many things to help yourself sleep better. The steps you take depend on the kind of difficulties you're having and the severity of the problem. Less severe sleep problems can usually be handled by following some commonsense tips. More severe problems may require the help of a family doctor or a specialist in sleep disorders.

What You Can Do

If you frequently experience insomnia, try these simple but highly effective techniques for promoting sleep.

Maintain a Consistent Sleep-Wake Schedule

Difficulty in falling asleep may be caused in part by a confusion of the internal body clock, the suprachiasmatic nucleus (SCN). The SCN resets itself constantly, based on the cycles of light and dark. If you're frequently exposed to light—even small amounts—late in the evening, your SCN might not be resetting itself properly. As a result, your brain may behave as if it's still daytime when it's time for bed. Resetting your SCN depends in large part on maintaining a consistent sleep-wake schedule.

Try to go to bed at the same time every night even if you're not tired. Pick a bedtime that takes your after-school and social schedules into account, but still allows adequate rest. For instance, you might decide that even if you don't get home from choir rehearsal until 9:00 P.M., you'll go to bed at 9:30. That's your bedtime, no matter what. No more staying up until 10:00 or 11:00 P.M. watching television. Set your bedtime, and stick to it.

Maintaining a consistent bedtime schedule helps your body clock learn when it should begin preparing to fall asleep. The SCN will eventually count on sleep occurring at a set time and will regulate the flow of melatonin and other sleep chemicals according to that schedule.

Try to wake up at the same time every day. For some people, keeping to a rigid wake schedule is more important than keeping to a strict bedtime schedule. Pick a wake-up time that fits your daily schedule. If you need to wake up at 6:00 A.M. during the week to catch the bus on time, then get up at 6:00 A.M. on weekends too.

Sleeping late on Saturday and Sunday resets your SCN to a later wake time. As a result, you'll be awake later in the evening and be more likely to have a hard time falling asleep. If you get up at 6:00 A.M., even on weekends, and get into bright light, you'll be helping your SCN reset itself properly. You'll be more likely to feel sleepy when it's time for bed, and you'll fall asleep more easily.

Set the Stage for Sleep

Some circumstances make it difficult to sleep. For instance, during hot or humid weather, many people either can't sleep or sleep very lightly. The ideal temperature for sleep is from 64 to 72 degrees Fahrenheit (17 to 22 degrees Celsius). Males tend to prefer cooler temperatures for sleep, while females tend to like warmer temperatures.

Apart from a comfortable temperature, sleep requires fatigue. It's extremely difficult to sleep unless you're tired, and it's impossible when you're not relaxed. If you're nervous about something or if you just finished exercising, you won't be able to fall asleep until you're more relaxed—physically and mentally.

Silence generally promotes sleep, but some people find low levels of repeating sounds relaxing. For instance, some people might play a tape or CD of waves lapping a seashore. The repeated sounds of the waves provide a pleasant background. People who live near busy streets, railroad tracks, or airports usually grow accustomed to the sounds of routine events, such as traffic going by, or a jet taking off.

Sounds unrelated to usual events may prevent sleep, however. A loud party in a quiet neighborhood, for example, can keep just about everyone in the area from sleeping. So can sounds that occur in an unpredictable pattern, such as the pounding of nails or the revving of an engine.

A soft, supportive surface is important for sleep. Most people sleep on a mattress, though some prefer a water bed. As long as you are comfortable and your body is well supported, the type of foundation—mattress or water bed—makes no real difference in the quality of sleep.

The position in which you sleep can affect how well you sleep, however. Some people can fall asleep sitting in a chair, but the sleep they get tends to be shorter and less refreshing than the sleep they would get if they were lying flat. The most refreshing sleep tends to occur when you sleep flat, with your head and neck supported by one or two pillows.

Let Sleep Come Naturally

If you have trouble sleeping one night, you'll probably have trouble the next night because you'll wonder whether you'll be able to fall asleep. And the more you wonder, the more you'll concentrate on falling asleep. And the more you concentrate on falling asleep, the less likely you'll be able to actually do so.

Some people with insomnia try to force themselves to sleep. They lie in bed with their eyes clamped shut, telling themselves to fall asleep. It doesn't work. Falling asleep happens only when you stop thinking about it.

Rather than trying to force yourself to sleep, work on reducing your level of alertness. Lower the lights or turn them off completely an hour or so before bedtime. Avoid physical activity of any kind for at least 2 hours before bedtime. Avoid caffeine and alcohol; both of these substances interfere with sleep. Plan your evening so that intense conversation and activities requiring mental alertness take place earlier in the evening.

Do all your nighttime rituals every night, such as brushing your teeth or putting on your pajamas. These little rituals help your body prepare for sleep.

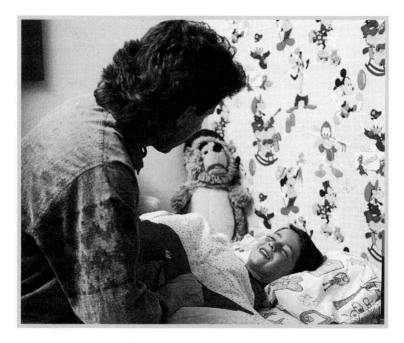

Maintaining the same bedtime routine each night can help set the stage for sleep.

If you frequently have trouble sleeping because you tend to worry about things, set aside 20 or 30 minutes in the evening as "worry time." Tell yourself that you'll use this time—and only this time—to worry. When you finish your worry period, allow yourself the luxury of not worrying at bedtime. After all, you've already done your worrying for the day! By looking at worrying as a task to be completed, you set yourself up for success on two fronts. First, you'll succeed by accomplishing a goal—worrying for a set period of time—and second, you'll fall asleep more easily because you'll be more relaxed.

Practice Relaxation Techniques

The old standby—counting sheep—really does help you fall asleep. Counting sheep (or pigs in pen, feathers on a bird, or tiles on the ceiling) is a repetitive task that can lull your senses and help bring on sleep.

Many sleep experts recommend **meditation** as a way to prepare for sleep. Meditation involves focusing your mind on a single image, usually of a peaceful place, such as the banks of a stream or the floor next to a warm fire. Certain forms of meditation involve silently repeating a particular word or phrase over and over.

Meditation is a simple exercise that, with practice, can be done at any time of the day. It helps you relax and can reduce stress. Try this basic meditation exercise to help you prepare for sleep.

1. Find a quiet place where you feel comfortable and won't be disturbed.
2. Remove all sources of noise or distraction. Shut off the television and radio, unplug the phone, and ask your family or friends not to disturb you for 30 minutes.
3. Sit comfortably in a chair, on the bed, or on a cushion on the floor. You might find the cross-legged position comfortable. In this position your legs are crossed and your hands rest gently

Meditation can help prepare you for sleep.

on your knees. Whichever position you choose, make sure that your head, neck, and back are in line and that you keep your back straight.

4. Close your eyes, and take a deep breath. Let the breath out slowly.
5. Count each breath in and each breath out. Repeat to yourself: "Inhale, one. Exhale, two. Inhale, three. Exhale four." Keep counting for 10 breaths ("Exhale, ten"). Then start again from one.
6. When you begin meditating, repeat this slow, rhythmic breathing for 5 minutes. Keep practicing until you can continue the breathing exercise for 20 minutes.

Another technique to reduce stress and promote sleep was developed by a physician named Edmund Jacobsen. **Progressive relaxation** involves the tightening and relaxing of different muscle groups in a certain sequence. Many people begin with muscles in the feet and toes, and then gradually work their way up to the face and neck. Others prefer to work from the face down. The direction doesn't matter. The important thing is to relax each muscle group, one after another.

Progressive relaxation can help you prepare for sleep, especially after a physically or emotionally demanding day. Here's how to do progressive relaxation.

1. Get ready for bed as you normally would, and then get into bed.
2. Breathe deeply, and clench your toes to tighten your foot and toe muscles.
3. Relax your toes as you breathe out slowly.
4. Breathe deeply, and clench the muscles of your lower leg. Concentrate on tightening just your calf, not your foot or thigh muscles. Try to keep your foot relaxed.
5. Relax your calf as you breathe out slowly.
6. Repeat this sequence as you clench and relax your thighs,

abdomen, buttocks, chest, forearms, hands, upper arms, and neck.

7. After the neck, clench and relax the muscles around your eyes and nose. Finally, do the same for your jaw, letting the jaw go completely slack as you breathe out.

8. Concentrate on the feelings you experience as you relax your muscles. You should feel yourself slip slowly into a state of deep relaxation.

If you enjoy writing in a diary or journal, you might benefit from jotting down some thoughts each evening before bed. Sit comfortably in bed, and support your back with a firm pillow. Summarize how you're feeling by writing it in a journal. Note anything that is worrying you. You might even note the steps you plan to take to deal with the things you're worried about.

Sometimes the act of writing about your problems allows you to release them from your mind. With fewer problems on your mind, you may then be able to fall asleep more easily.

When You Need Help

Some sleep disorders require medical attention. For instance, narcolepsy is a serious disorder that is treated with prescription drugs. Other disorders that should receive medical attention include sleep apnea, severe restless leg syndrome, and severe snoring.

Drugs are commonly used to treat these and other sleep disorders. In addition, a growing number of nondrug therapies are proving useful, particularly for sleep apnea and snoring.

Drugs that Promote Sleep
A number of drugs can be used to bring on, or induce, sleep. Several sleep-inducing drugs, such as Sominex, Nytol, and Unisom, are available at pharmacies and grocery stores. Most of these

drugs contain either doxylamine or diphenhydramine, chemicals that belong to a group of drugs called antihistamines. Antihistamines dry the throat and nose and are commonly used in cold remedies. They also cause drowsiness, which makes them effective sleep-inducing drugs. Their effectiveness tends to wear off quickly though. In addition, these drugs may cause dizziness, stomach upset, and dryness of the nose and mouth. Over-the-counter sleeping aids may help you get to sleep, they may also cause you to wake up in the middle of the night. For these reasons, it's a good idea to avoid using them.

A number of herbal remedies that help induce sleep are also available. Melatonin is a key chemical in the body's control of the sleep-wake cycle. Herbal melatonin may enhance your body's own supply of the chemical and thus, promote sleep. Some studies indicate that melatonin may also be useful for reducing the effects of jet lag in travelers.

Chamomile, a flower used in herbal tea, seems to relax people and reduce alertness. In one study, chamomile helped induce

Chamomile tea, made from chamomile plants, may help you relax at bedtime.

deep sleep in patients who were undergoing a painful study of the arteries of the heart. Some people find that drinking a cup of chamomile tea helps them to fall asleep.

Like chamomile, valerian has also been used to promote sleep, but few scientific studies support its use as a sleeping aid. Other herbal medicines used to promote sleep include tryptophan, lemon balm, fennel, rosemary, hops, pennyroyal, and marjoram. In Germany, many people combine anise, honey, and warm milk in a bedtime drink. The Hopi Indians of the southwestern United States often use an herb called sand verbena to induce sleep.

Drugs that require a doctor's prescription are generally reserved for people with severe, prolonged insomnia and certain sleep disorders. Doctors can select from a wide variety of drugs to treat insomnia, including hypnotics, such as chloral hydrate and zolpidem, and tranquilizers, such as flurazepam and triazolam. These drugs work largely by causing a dampening effect on nerve signals traveling through the brain and spinal cord. The dampening causes drowsiness and a feeling of relaxation.

Many hypnotics and tranquilizers change the quality of sleep. For example, many prescription sleeping aids cause the individual to spend more time in Stage 2 sleep (light sleep) and considerably less time in dream sleep and Stages 3 and 4 sleep (deep sleep). Shortened periods of these Stages may lead to daytime drowsiness and an inability to wake up quickly in the morning, a condition commonly referred to as a **hangover.**

Hypnotics and sedatives can also lead to **dependence,** a condition in which the individual relies on a drug and may be uncomfortable without it. In addition, because hypnotics and sedatives tend to work effectively for only short periods of time, the individual usually ends up taking more and more of the drug to get the same sleep-inducing effect.

When a person finally stops taking the drug, a condition known as rebound insomnia may occur. Rebound insomnia is a return to sleeplessness following the use of a sedative or hypnotic. Rebound insomnia is sometimes worse than the original condition and may last several weeks, depending on how long the sedative or hypnotic was used.

Evaluation at a Sleep Center

Anyone who has severe trouble sleeping and who repeatedly experiences sleep deprivation should seek medical attention. People with severe, prolonged insomnia should be fully evaluated at a certified sleep center to determine the cause of the insomnia and the best treatment for it.

Doctors at a sleep center can monitor the individual's heart rate, breathing rate, brain-wave patterns, and other vital signs during sleep. Evaluation of these signs can help doctors determine whether the individual has simple insomnia or a more complex condition that requires intensive treatment.

Chapter 6

In Your Dreams

Dreaming is an adventure you can count on having every night. After you go to sleep tonight, you'll dream. You may not remember it, but you will dream. Maybe you'll dream that you're flying through the hallways at school or crossing the finish line in a big race. Maybe you'll dream that you're in a strange new place, surrounded by people you don't know, and you are telling those people about a new CD you just bought. Sometimes the dreams you have will make sense to you. At other times, your dreams might seem like little more than random collections of events.

Dream History

The significance of dreams has mystified people through the ages. Nearly 4,000 years ago, emotionally disturbed Egyptians would sleep in a special temple. When they awoke, they told their dreams to a priest. The priest interpreted the dreams and advised the people on how to solve their problems.

Ancient Greeks also interpreted dreams and tried to use the interpretations to heal sick people. Greeks who were sick would stay at special sleep temples until they had a dream that seemed to promise a return to health. It wasn't uncommon for these patients to stay weeks or even months at the temples, waiting to dream about a cure.

In the Roman Empire, a famous physician named Galen of Pergamum once used dreams to "cure" a man of a lung condition called pleurisy. The man dreamed that the top of his head was covered with blood. So Galen decided that the man was "in need of a liberal bloodletting." Galen drained a large amount of blood from the patient and pronounced him cured.

In some religions, dreams were considered the work of the devil. During the Middle Ages, for example, the Roman Catholic Church held that a vision revealed to an individual in a dream was evil and, therefore, a sin. At least two native peoples—the Inuit of Hudson Bay in Canada and the Patani Malay of Indonesia— believe that dreams are linked to the soul. They believe the soul leaves the body during sleep and that someone awakened during sleep risks losing his or her soul.

The great Greek philosopher Aristotle was the first person to consider dreams as memories of the day's events, rather than divine messages. Modern-day research into dreams began with the famous psychoanalyst Sigmund Freud. Freud believed dreams reveal deep-seated feelings that the dreamer doesn't want to recognize. The brain, Freud believed, uses dreams to hide these feelings from the conscious mind. Although many of Freud's theories have since been disproved, the advances he made into the understanding of dreams and their meaning continue to influence dream research today.

Not everyone is convinced that dreams are trying to tell us something. A few prominent sleep researchers believe dreams are just the random, meaningless result of the brain's attempt to make sense of incoming electrical signals.

Psychoanalyst Sigmund Freud pioneered modern research into dreams and their interpretation.

Dream Messages

Most sleep researchers believe that every dream you have carries a message of some kind. The meaning of the message may be immediately clear to you, or it might require some thought to figure out. Dream messages often come wrapped in confusing packages. You might dream, for example, that you're in a room full of birds. You jump out of a window only to find yourself sitting at your desk at school, talking with a friend. You might then suddenly find yourself on a boat in the middle of the sea, paddling furiously for shore. It may be difficult to make sense of such a baffling dream.

With practice it becomes easier to understand the meaning of dreams. Many dreams involve one or more basic elements that can help the dreamer analyze the dream more accurately. Those elements include person, place, color, mood, and the role (if any) played by animals.

The Cast of Characters

You probably play a major role in most or all of your dreams, but you might not always recognize yourself. In your dreams, you could be another person, an animal, or even an object. Analyzing such dreams is difficult. Try to put yourself in the place of the person, animal, or object you believe represents you. Perhaps you believe that the automobile tire rolling down the street in your dream is actually you! Putting yourself in the tire's place might lead you to the conclusion that you feel like you're constantly on the run.

The Setting

The place in which your dream occurs may be important. If you dream you are in a pool, ask yourself whether the water was cold. If so, your dream might be telling you to "cool it" about something you're thinking about doing. Maybe you dream about being trapped in a hot, stuffy closet. Could your dream be telling you that a relationship in your life is stifling you? Considering the dream's atmosphere and location can help you gain insight into its meaning.

Color

Many people dream in vivid colors. People who dream in color tend to be highly aware of color in their waking life. People less aware of color in their waking life are less likely to have multi-colored dreams.

Whether you dream in vivid colors, only one color, or in black-and-white, isn't as important as what part a particular color plays in a dream. If you normally dream in black-and-white and one night you have a dream in which you're rowing down a bright green river, the color of the river might be important.

Mood

The mood created in a dream can shed light on the meaning of the dream. If you remember feeling sad during a dream, for example, but you aren't sure why, try to relate the emotion to events in your life. Did you get a poor grade on a recent test? Maybe you are sad or disappointed that you didn't do better. Your dream may be telling you that you're still upset and that you need to deal with your disappointment more effectively.

Animals

Animals usually represent fears, desires, or basic human needs. An animal that figures prominently in a dream may represent a deep-seated fear or emotion you need to deal with. For instance, if a bat plays an important role in one of your dreams, you might ask yourself whether you've been avoiding a problem in your waking life. Have you been behaving, in other words, as if you're as "blind as a bat"?

Remembering Your Dreams

Like most people, you probably don't remember most of your dreams. They occur too early in the night or they are not vivid or disturbing enough to wake you up so that you can remember them.

Most of the dreams you remember occur shortly before you awaken.

Normally, the memory of a dream is stored in a short-term memory area in the brain. Unless the brain moves the memory quickly—within a minute or two—out of this short-term area and into a brain area where the memory can stay longer, the memory disappears. If you awaken shortly after your dream, though, and write about the dream or describe it to someone right away, you can push the dream into long-term memory and recall it more easily later.

Some people say they never dream. Experts say that everyone dreams, whether or not they think they do. People who say they don't dream may not recall their dreams easily, and so mistakenly believe that they don't dream at all.

About once every 4 or 5 days, most adults can recall a dream. The ability to recall dreams is a skill that can be learned. One of the best ways to learn to remember dreams more easily is simply to tell yourself to do so.

As you lie in bed preparing to fall asleep, repeat to yourself, "I'll dream tonight and I'll remember it when I wake up." Telling yourself to remember your dreams somehow prepares your mind to recall your dreams later.

Ask Your Dreams

If you're having difficulty remembering your dreams, ask your dreams why you don't remember them. That may sound like an odd technique, but it works. The technique, originally developed by psychotherapist Frederick Perls, involves a bit of role-playing.

Place two chairs opposite each other. Sit in one chair and imagine that the dreams you can't remember are sitting in the other. Ask your dreams, "Why can't I remember you? I want to remember you but you won't let me. Why not?"

Then switch chairs and answer your own questions. Perhaps

you'll say, "Because you were too tired last night," or "Because you forgot," or even "I don't know. Why do you think I didn't let you remember the dreams?" According to the theory, having this kind of role-playing discussion with yourself will help you remember your dreams more readily.

You can use the same technique if you remember a dream but can't figure out what it means. Ask your dream, "Why can't I understand what you mean?" Or you might tell your dream, "Your message isn't clear enough. Can't you give me something simpler?" When you dream that night, you'll be more likely to remember your dreams the next morning.

Lying in bed for a few moments after you wake up might also help you remember your dreams. This gives your mind a chance to dip into its memory bank and recall pieces of a dream. Try to think about the feelings you experienced and the thoughts you had at the moment you woke up. Then try to work your way backward. This method works particularly well if an alarm clock awakened you.

Recording Your Dreams

Recording your dreams can help you remember them in more detail, and that might help you interpret them. Keep some paper and a pen—or a tape recorder—next to your bed. You might keep a flashlight by the bed too, in case you wake up in the middle of the night and don't want to turn on a light.

When you first wake up with the memory of a dream in your mind, don't start writing or speaking into the tape recorder yet. First, lie still and try to hold on to the feelings you experienced in the dream. Try to picture where the dream took place. Listen for the sounds you heard. Try to place yourself in the dream again. Don't force yourself to remember a dream, that will almost guarantee that you won't remember. Try quietly allowing the dream experience to return on its own.

After you've put yourself back into your dream and you feel

confident enough to record it, reach for the pen and paper (or tape recorder) and record some key words about the dream. Focus on the most vivid, important images. You don't need to describe the dream in detail yet. Just recording key words will help jog your memory about the dream later and allow you to record more details when you're more awake.

When you wake up in the morning, read over the key words and fill in the parts of the dream that you can remember. If you recorded a few key words about a vivid dream the night before, but you can't remember the dream in the morning, you might still be able to retrieve the dream from your memory. Read the key words a few times and then go on about your daily business. A word or image you come across later in the day may jog your memory and allow you to recall the dream you thought you had forgotten.

Using A Dream Diary

To help you keep track of your dreams, consider using a dream diary. In a dream diary, you write a description of your dream on one page and your interpretation of it on the opposite page. Date each page so that you know when the dream occurred. Describe how the dream made you feel. For instance, one dream may be peaceful and quiet and make you feel calm; another may be busy and full of images that make you feel excited and happy.

Do you remember any colors in your dream? If you dreamed about being in a forest, green would probably be a prominent color. If you were in a forest and the main colors were red and yellow, color might be telling you something important.

Try to identify what event, thought, or feeling might have triggered the dream. If you dreamed that someone kept pulling at your foot, can you identify what action or event might have triggered that image? Perhaps you injured your toe a few days ago and you still have a bandage on it. If so, the dream might have been triggered by your injury. If you can identify a dream trigger, jot it down as well.

Describe your dream in as much detail as possible. Finally, sum up your dream in just a few words. If you have trouble summarizing the dream, write a title for it. That might help you identify the most important part of the dream. After you've described the dream and summarized it in a title or short sentence, you're ready to interpret it.

Interpreting the Dream

Dream interpretation is not easy. The only person who can really know what one of your dreams means is you. The interpretations in this book—or in any book about dream interpretation, for that matter—can offer only general guidelines about what your particular dreams might mean.

The images and activities you see in a dream might not always be what they seem. A tree may actually be a dream image of your

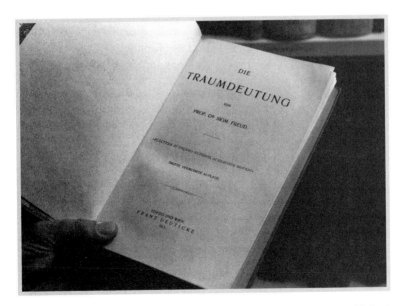

Sigmund Freud's landmark book, The Interpretation of Dreams, *published in 1900, sparked intense interest in dream research. Freud called dreams "the royal road to a knowledge of the unconscious activities of the mind."*

family. A window may be a dream image of your eyes. Climbing a mountain may have nothing to do with climbing or mountains but everything to do with struggling with a difficult problem. Consider many possible meanings of key objects or activities in your dream to interpret the dream correctly.

As you review a dream, try to identify its most important characteristics. Perhaps the color red played a strong role, or trees, or a weapon. For example, suppose you dream about a black lion sitting on your bedroom window ledge. Dream interpretation books say that the color of the cat—black—may indicate that you're sad about something or someone close to you. A lion in a dream typically indicates courage or strength of character. You could interpret the dream as saying that you're sad about someone you consider to be brave and strong.

In reality, you might have a better explanation for the dream yourself. You may know, for instance, that your black cat, Sam, enjoys jumping on you whenever you lie down. Perhaps that afternoon, Sam jumped onto your belly while you were lying on the couch, watching TV. In that case, your dream would be a reflection of what happened that afternoon and it doesn't mean that you're sad about a courageous friend. Only you would be able to provide those explanations; no book could do that.

As you practice recording and interpreting your dreams over time, maybe you'll notice some patterns taking shape. Recognizing those patterns might help you interpret your dreams. For instance, do you always have the same dream the night before a big exam? Dream interpretation is not an exact science, but with practice you might be able to decode some of the messages in your dreams. The dream encyclopedia, found in the Appendix, lists some common dream themes and their possible meaning. See if you recognize some of them from your dreams.

Glossary

adrenocorticotropic hormone (ACTH)—a chemical that plays a key role in the body's response to stress or its preparation for it

alpha waves—slow, regular brain waves that occur during Stage 1 sleep

amygdala—an almond-shaped clump of brain tissue that plays a key role in memory and emotions

antihistamine—a chemical that blocks the action of histamines in the body. It dries the membranes of the mouth and nose and causes drowsiness

beta waves—small, rapid brain waves that occur during periods of alertness

bruxism—teeth grinding during sleep

cataplexy—sudden paralysis of the muscles of the body that occurs in some patients with narcolepsy

circadian rhythm—natural body rhythms that occur once every 24 hours

continuous positive airway pressure (CPAP)—a method of keeping the upper airway open during sleep in which oxygen flows constantly into the lungs and helps to prevent snoring

cryptochrome—a chemical in the eye that absorbs blue light and transfers signals to the brain's sleep center

deep sleep—a period of total calm and comfort during sleep; also called Stage 4 sleep

delta waves—large, slow brain waves that occur during periods of deep sleep

dependence—being reliant on a drug; feeling an urge to take a drug to experience its effects or avoid the effects caused by its absence

dream sleep—a period during which vivid dreams occur; also called REM sleep

electroencephalogram (EEG)—a recording of brain-wave activity

electroencephalograph—a machine for detecting and recording brain waves

growth hormone—a body chemical produced by the pituitary gland that promotes the growth of all body tissues

hangover—a condition in which the individual feels drowsy during the day and is unable to awaken quickly in the morning

immune system—the body's infection-fighting system, comprised of white blood cells, platelets, lymph fluid, and other components

induce—to bring on or start

insomnia—an inability to fall asleep or stay asleep

jet lag—a condition in which the body clock becomes confused as a result of flying across several time zones within a short period of time

lark—type of individual who tends to function best in the morning hours

laser-assisted uvulopalatoplasty (LAUP)—a procedure in which doctors use a laser to trim the uvula, tonsils, and soft palate to reduce snoring

lux—a measurement of the brightness of light

meditation—a form of relaxation in which the individual focuses on an image of a calm, quiet place

melatonin—a body chemical produced by the pineal gland and responsible for signaling body cells to slow their activities

microsleep—a sudden, brief period of Stage 1 sleep that occurs during periods of drowsiness

narcolepsy—a sleep disorder in which a person may fall uncontrollably asleep at any time

obese—excessively fat

obstructive sleep apnea—lack of breathing caused by a restricted air flow

on call—a work assignment in which the person can be called to work at any time

optic nerve—the major nerve leading from the eye to the brain

owl—type of individual who tends to function best in the evening

periodic limb movement disorder (PLMD)—a condition similar to restless leg syndrome in which the arms and legs tend to flail uncontrollably during sleep

pineal gland—a small clump of tissue located deep inside the brain that produces melatonin

pituitary gland—a clump of tissue located deep inside the brain that releases a number of key body chemicals

pleurisy—inflammation of the lining covering the surface of the lungs

progressive relaxation—a stress-reduction technique that involves conscious relaxation of muscle groups in sequence

rapid eye movements (REM)—jerky movements of the eye that signal dream sleep

rebound insomnia—insomnia that follows the use of a sleeping aid

reconditioning therapy—form of relaxation therapy in which the individual avoids doing things that signal wakefulness instead of sleepiness

REM sleep—the period of sleep during which vivid dreams occur; rapid eye movement sleep

rotating shifts—a work schedule in which an individual works one shift for a while and then is rotated to another shift

shift work—work scheduled at times other than the traditional eight-hour (daylight) time frame

sleep debt—a buildup of missed sleep

sleep deprivation—a lack of sleep

soft palate—the fleshy part of the roof of the mouth

somnoplasty—a form of surgery that uses radiowaves to remove excess tissues in the throat and reduce snoring

Stage 1 sleep—the period of lightest sleep in which the individual feels calm, comfortable, and peaceful

Stage 2 sleep—the period of sleep in which it becomes difficult to awaken the individual

Stage 3 sleep—the transition period between Stage 2 sleep and Stage 4 sleep

Stage 4 sleep—the period of deep sleep

Stage 5 sleep—the period of dream sleep

stimulus control—a type of therapy used to treat insomnia, in which a person avoids doing things that signal wakefulness

suprachiasmatic nucleus (SCN)—a group of nerve cells inside the brain that act as the body clock

thalamus—a section of the brain that acts as a relay station for nerve signals passing between the brain and the spinal cord

theta waves—deep, slow brain waves that occur during Stage 2 sleep

time zones—regions of the world divided along imaginary north-to-south lines; time varies by one hour between each two zones

tonsils—clumps of lymphatic tissue on each side of the back of the mouth

unihemispheric sleep—a phenomenon seen in animals in which one half of the brain falls asleep while the other half remains awake

uvula—a small lobe of tissue hanging from the palate in the mouth

Dream Encyclopedia

What does it mean if you dream about your dog or cat? How about if you dream about a wedding or a birth? What if you dream that you're flying, swimming, or falling from a tall building? Interpreting your dreams can be fun, interesting, and sometimes helpful. Dreams might help you solve a problem or shed light on your personal relationships. Dreams may also reflect what you wish would happen in real life.

If everyone in the world had the same dream, the interpretations of that dream would be as varied as the people who had the dream. Your personal experiences are reflected in your dreams, so take them into account when you are trying to interpret your dreams. However, some common themes that occur in many people's dreams, and dream researchers have offered some interpretations of those themes. Some of them are listed below.

Acting on Stage

In the comedy *As You Like It* Shakespeare wrote, "All the world's a stage and all the men and women merely players." That's true in the dream world as well. If you dream you're acting on a stage, that may mean that in your waking world you're pretending to be someone or something you're not. You may be concerned about your appearance or about how your friends see you. Are you hoping to earn their applause? If you forget your lines in a dream, it may mean that you feel insecure or uncertain about something in your waking life.

Anger or Hostility

If you express anger or hostility toward another person in a dream, it may mean that you are angry with yourself or that you are feeling an emotion in your waking life that you haven't been able to control. It could also mean that you are truly angry at that person!

Arguments

Having an argument with another person in a dream doesn't necessarily mean that you are angry with that person. It may instead indicate that two sides of your own personality aren't in agreement. Perhaps you are unsure about a decision you need to make. Knowing who won your dream argument may help make your decision easier.

Bats

If you dream about a bat, it may mean that you're not seeing something you should be seeing in your waking life. (Are you being "blind as a bat"?) Bats may also indicate a keen sense of direction. If you dreamed about bats after you made an important decision, maybe the bats are telling you that you made the right decision.

Being Chased

Chasing someone or being chased is a common occurrence in dreams. Being chased often signifies a fear of something. Perhaps you're afraid that you aren't prepared for an upcoming test. To learn what a chase dream means, you have to turn and face whatever is chasing you. Before falling asleep the night after a chasing dream, tell yourself to turn and face your pursuer. Demand to know why you're being chased. If you can face your pursuer in a dream, you may find it easier to face fears in your waking life.

Birds

A bird in flight may serve as a symbol of freedom. Imagine a hawk, flying far above a meadow. Dreaming about a hawk might mean that you need to take a look at a problem or a situation differently, from a distance.

Birth

Dreams about giving birth can signify many different things. Maybe you have a desire to have a child, or perhaps you are proud that you worked hard to finish a project or assignment. Birth dreams are generally encouraging and often signify joy or hope about the future.

Buildings

If you dream that you're exploring a building, the dream may be encouraging you to explore your own personality. Parts of the building may also have meaning. Windows may represent the eyes. A staircase may represent progress you're making on a project or assignment. A door may have several meanings, depending on whether it's opening or closing or whether you're going in or out. A door closing on you may mean that you're shutting something out of your waking life.

Calculations

If you dream about working out a complex math problem or taking a measurement, it may mean that you're wrestling with a decision in your waking life. Perhaps there's a calculation you've left out of your decision you've been trying to make.

Cars

Cars may represent power or skill in using your hands or a desire to get ahead in life. If you're having trouble steering a car, it may mean that you're feeling out of control about something. Running out of fuel may indicate that you're tired and "running out of gas." Can't get the car into gear? Perhaps you're struggling with a problem you haven't been able to solve.

Cliffs, Mountains, Ditches, or Gorges

Climbing up a cliff or mountain in a dream or coming upon a deep ditch or wide gorge may mean that you're facing a problem in your waking life that needs to be solved. If you reach the top of the mountain in your dream or successfully cross the gorge, it may mean that you're committed to solving the problem, or perhaps that you already have.

Clothing

Clothing dreams are common and typically point out how the dreamer feels about his or her own appearance. If you're dressed in worn old clothes and everyone else in your dream is well dressed, it may mean that you feel insecure among your friends or co-workers. Wearing an apron or hat in a dream may indicate that you're covering something up or doing something you think you shouldn't be doing.

If you're dressed in uncomfortable clothing, it may mean that you're unhappy or irritated with something in your waking life. Perhaps you dislike one of your courses in school or you hate your job. If you don't have clothes on, it may mean that you feel unprotected in your waking life. Perhaps you feel insecure about something you're doing or feel as if other people are picking on you. Perhaps you felt embarrassed recently. Being naked in a dream may reflect your insecurity or embarrassment.

Colors

A predominantly red dream may mean that you're angry about something. Red may also indicate passion or energy. Yellow and orange are usually cheerful colors. Blue might reflect the dreamer's inner mood. If the blue is a dark shade, it may indicate that you're feeling sad or lonely. If it's a light shade, it may indicate that you're feeling hopeful. Green could be a symbol of the outdoors, or it may mean that you're jealous about something.

Deafness or Blindness
Dreaming that you're deaf or blind doesn't mean that you're about to lose the ability to hear or see. It may mean that you're not hearing what someone in your waking life is trying to tell you or that you're not seeing something important.

Death
Although dreams about death are common, they rarely represent the death of someone in the dreamer's waking life. Most dreams about death indicate change or rebirth. Dreaming about a coffin being lowered into the ground may mean you are about to make a change in your waking life. Dreams about death often occur around the time of a marriage or divorce. If you dream that you have died, it may mean that you've shed yourself of a long-held belief or bias.

Falling
Dreams about falling are common and usually linked to fear. A dream about falling might mean that the dreamer feels insecure about having to deliver a speech, for instance. A falling dream may also mean that someone in your waking life is "on the rise." If a friend moves up in status, you might feel as if you've fallen in status. Falling might also signify a loss of control in your waking life or a feeling of helplessness.

Fences or other Boundaries
A fence, gate, or other boundary may represent a challenge you are struggling with in your waking life. Boundaries may also signify a feeling of being restricted from doing what you want to do.

Figure Skating or Dancing

A dream about dancing or figure skating may mean that you're enjoying life. If you felt out of control when you were dancing or skating, it might mean that you've been acting carelessly in your waking life. If you were stepping on your dream partner's toes, it might mean that you've been interfering with someone in your waking life.

Fire

The meaning of fire depends in part on the nature of the fire and the atmosphere of the dream. A cozy fire in a fireplace may represent something personal in your life. A bonfire, on the other hand, might signify a message you need to communicate to a group of people. In any case, fire frequently indicates an intense emotion. If the fire in your dream was nothing more than a candle you blew out, the flame may represent a relationship with a friend or a particularly emotional time. Blowing the candle out might indicate that you recently ended the relationship or have worked through difficulties in your waking life.

Flowers

Flowers are linked to friendship, love, and warm feelings (think about giving someone a bouquet). Giving a bouquet of flowers to someone may indicate that you love or respect the person receiving the flowers. If a person in your dreams gives *you* flowers, it may mean that you think the person is fond of you. Either way, determining who the person is could help you identify someone you have hidden feelings for or someone you think might have hidden feelings for you.

The type of flowers that appear in your dream may also be important. Wildflowers are often associated with natural, down-to-earth qualities. Buttercups may be a symbol of childhood. Orchids usually indicate beauty and wealth. Lilies may suggest rebirth or innocence.

Flying

Flying is one of the most common dream themes, and it can take many forms. You might find yourself soaring through the sky like an eagle, floating in a hot-air balloon, or zooming along a few feet above the ground. Flying in a dream might mean that you recently succeeded in a project or assignment in your waking life. It may also mean that you're trying to rise above a problem. If you feel out of control when you fly, it may mean that you've lost control of something in your waking life.

Food

If you're eating in your dreams—another common dream activity—you may simply be hungry! The food may also represent an object you wish belonged to you. An apple may signify something you did wrong (remember the apple Eve gave Adam?). Apples may also represent wisdom.

Giving a Speech

Giving a speech in a dream may be an expression of your need to state an opinion. If your dream audience applauded or otherwise liked what you had to say, it may mean that your opinion will be well received in your waking life.

Injuries

Dreaming of an injury may indicate that an illness or injury actually exists. Dreaming that you've lost a great deal of blood may mean that your body doesn't have enough vitamins and minerals. A dream that your hand is injured or disabled may signify an inability to perform a task.

Dreams about feet often relate to the progress you're making in some part of your waking life. Have you been "dragging your feet" about a problem? Dreaming of an ear may be a signal that you should listen to someone's advice. Losing your teeth—a common dream event—is usually linked to concerns about self-image.

Lawyers, Judges, and other Law-Enforcement Officials
A dream in which you're a lawyer, judge, or a police officer in a courtroom may relate to a moral dilemma you're facing. Maybe your best friend shoplifted a wallet. You might feel torn between loyalty for your friend and your knowledge that shoplifting is wrong. If you're the judge in the dream, is there someone in your waking life waiting for you to make a judgment?

Losing a Body Part
Losing your teeth, hair, or an arm or a leg in a dream is often a symbol of something missing in your life. For instance, if a close friend turned his back on you recently, you might dream that you've lost your right arm. Losing your teeth may be a symbol of feeling insecure in your waking life.

Marriage
Dreaming about a future husband or wife isn't a prediction of who you'll marry. Instead, it may represent something you hope will happen. It may also be a symbol of your desire to join a group or your need to blend several different ideas into one. If you dream that you're married to more than one person, it may mean that you're involved in too many activities in your waking life. Your dream may be telling you to cut back, or divorce yourself, from some activities or responsibilities.

Mazes
Stuck in a maze in one of your dreams? The maze may represent a complex problem you're dealing with. The dream may be telling you to make sure you give the problem more thought or planning.

Mirrors
If you dream you are looking at yourself in a mirror, you may be wondering how others see you or you may be concerned about your appearance. Your dream may be telling you to try to see yourself as others see you.

Music

If music is an important part of your waking life you may hear music in your dreams. Many composers and songwriters have heard music in their dreams. Paul McCartney is said to have heard the tune for one of the *Beatles'* most famous songs, "Yesterday," in a dream.

The type of music isn't as important as other factors in interpreting the dream. If you dream that you're playing the piano alone in front of an audience, it may mean that you feel as if you're on your own or going solo in your waking life. Playing a trumpet or cymbals may indicate you are preparing to make an announcement.

Natural Disasters

Were you being hammered by a hurricane, lost in a storm at sea, or shaking in your shoes during an earthquake? If these or other natural disasters show up in a dream that may mean you're worried about losing control in your waking life. A life preserver or a beacon of light from a lighthouse may signal that there's hope!

Paralysis

Feeling paralyzed in a dream may mean that you feel paralyzed in your waking life as well. Perhaps you're unsure about a decision so you've been avoiding making it. Or you may feel helpless about a problem in your waking life. The paralysis of your dream may reflect the paralysis of your emotions in your waking life.

Pets

Most dreams with animals involve pets, such as dogs, cats, and horses. The meaning of an animal dream varies widely and depends on your view of that particular animal. To some people, horses represent emotional balance and inner strength. To others, they might represent discipline, artistry, or freedom.

Cats may be associated with cleverness or wisdom. Dogs are often linked to friendship, loyalty, and obedience. They may also represent fear or distrust. The actions of the dream dog can help you determine its meaning. If the dog in your dream is foaming at the mouth and attacking you, it may indicate that you don't trust someone close to you.

Playing on a Team
If you find yourself playing baseball, football, soccer, or another team sport in your dream, pay attention to what you and your teammates are doing. If everyone is working well together, it may mean that a team you're on in your waking life—such as your family, co-workers, or a team of students at school—is also getting along well and working together. If the players on your dream team are arguing with each other or feeling jealous of one player's talents, it may mean that the people on a team in your waking life are also not getting along well.

Punishments
Dreams often bring to light things that the dreamer knows but doesn't want to recognize. If you're being punished in a dream— maybe you're being sent to jail, beaten with a stick, or even hung by a mob—it may mean that you know you should be punished for something you've done. The punishment may also indicate that someone else deserves to be punished.

Referees or Umpires
Referees and umpires often represent a person of authority in your waking life. What happens in the dream may reflect your relationship with that person. For instance, ignoring a referee or umpire may indicate that you've been ignoring an authority figure—a teacher, perhaps, or a parent. Arguing with a call made by a referee or umpire may indicate that you disagree with a decision made by an authority figure in your waking life.

Taking a Test

Picture this: You're taking a test but all of the questions are in a foreign language. Or maybe you can't find the examination room and you waste the whole exam period looking for the right room. Test-taking dreams like these often indicate that you're facing a test in your waking life and that you're feeling insecure about it.

Telephones

If a telephone appears in a dream, it probably signals a need to communicate. If you were talking on the phone, can you identify who you've been talking to in your waking life? Perhaps you need to tell the person something. Or you may need help for something in your waking life and the telephone is signaling that you need assistance.

Trees

Think of the shape of a tree and you can begin to understand what trees might mean if they play a prominent role in your dreams. With its roots underground, a tree's branches extend outward from its main trunk. The branches keep dividing until they become leaf-covered twigs. Trees in a dream often represent a dreamer's family. Leaves or birds in a tree may represent the thoughts of the dreamer. The roots of the tree may be telling you something about your past.

Some experts say trees signify wisdom and strength. An oak tree may be a symbol of something that will last forever or something stable in your life.

Walking, Running, or Jogging

Walking, running, or jogging in a dream may signal how quickly or slowly your life is moving at the time. If you've been extremely busy and feel as if you're running on a treadmill, it wouldn't be surprising if you found yourself running or jogging in a dream. If you've been bored lately, you might dream that you're strolling slowly along a forest trail.

Walking, running, or jogging in a dream might also mean that you need more exercise. It's as if your mind is using a dream to say, "Get off the couch and get some exercise!"

Water

Before you were born, you floated in a watery fluid inside your mother's womb. The fluid protected and nourished you, and played an important role in your development and survival. A dream in which you're floating peacefully in calm, warm water may mean that you're comfortable and secure in your waking life.

However, a dream in which you're bobbing up and down in rough seas may indicate that you feel insecure, afraid, or that your life is tumbling out of control. Holding a dream umbrella to protect yourself against the rain may indicate that you're afraid to deal with a deep emotion. Swimming in a pool, on the other hand, may be a message about the importance of taking time to relax and have fun.

To Find Out More

Books

Ball, Nigel and Nick Hough. *The Sleep Solution: A 21-Night Program for Restful Sleep*. Berkeley: Ulysses Press, 1998.

Buchman, Dian Dincin, Ph.D. *The Complete Guide to Natural Sleep*. New Canaan, Connecticut: Keats Publishing, Inc., 1997.

Caldwell, J. Paul, M.D. *Sleep: Everything You Need to Know*. Buffalo: Firefly Books Inc., 1997.

Lavie, Peretz. *The Enchanted World of Sleep*. New Haven: Yale University Press, 1996.

Moore-Ede, M.D., Ph.D. and Suzanne LeVert. *The Complete Idiot's Guide to Getting a Good Night's Sleep*. New York: Macmillan Publishing United States, 1998.

Parker, Derek and Julia Parker. *Parkers' Complete Book of Dreams: The Definitive Guide to the Meaning of Dreams*. New York: Dorling Kindersley Publishing, Inc., 1995.

Pliskin, Marci and Shari L. Just, Ph.D. *The Complete Idiot's Guide to Interpreting Your Dreams*. New York: Macmillan Publishing United States, 1999.

Simpson, Carolyn. *Coping with Sleep Disorders*. New York: The Rosen Publishing Group, Inc., 1996.

Soccolich, R. M. *Night Symbols: 11,000 Dreams and Interpretations*. Long Island City, New York: Seaburn Publishing, 1998.

Wilson, Virginia N. *Sleep Thief: Restless Legs Syndrome*. Orange Park, Florida: Galaxy Books, 1996.

Organizations and Online Sites

American Academy of Sleep Medicine
6301 Bandel Road, Suite 101
Rochester, MN 55901
www.asda.org
The American Academy of Sleep Medicine is a professional organization made up of thousands of experts working in sleep centers throughout the United States. Its Internet site offers information for the general public advice about sleep and sleep disorders, and advice on getting a good night's sleep.

American Sleep Apnea Association
2025 Pennsylvania Avenue NW, Suite 905
Washington, DC 20006
www.sleepapnea.org
This organization is dedicated to helping people with sleep apnea and maintains a network of support groups in nearly every state.

Association for the Study of Dreams
www.asdreams.org
This site offers information and open discussions about dreams and dream science.

Circadian.com
www.circadian.com
This site provides information about the effects of shift work. It also offers an online test for users who want to know whether they're larks or owls.

Dream Central
www.sleeps.com
An independent site that offers information on dream interpretation, a dream dictionary, and an open discussion area.

Narcolepsy Network
10921 Reed Hartman Highway
Cincinnati, OH 45242
www.websciences.org/narnet
This organization of people with narcolepsy offers support to those with the disorder.

National Sleep Foundation
729 Fifteenth Street NW, Fourth Floor
Washington, DC 20005
www.sleepfoundation.org
This nonprofit organization provides information about sleep and support for people with sleep disorders.

Restless Leg Syndrome Foundation
www.rls.org
This site provides information about restless leg syndrome and publishes a quarterly newsletter called NightWalkers.

Sleepnet.com

www.sleepnet.com

This site offers dozens of links to other sleep-related Web sites. It also offers a special section for children with sleep disorders.

Index

About the Author

Andrew T. McPhee is a managing editor at Springhouse Corporation, an international publisher of reference materials for nurses and doctors. He was formerly an editor at Weekly Reader Corporation. Mr. McPhee graduated with a nursing degree from the University of New Hampshire in 1975.

Mr. McPhee has written or edited more than 700 health and life science articles for kids and has had articles published in *Nursing, RN, The Hartford Courant, Los Angeles Times, Washington Post, Moody Monthly, Countdown, Countdown for Kids, Weekly Reader, Current Science, U*S* Kids,* and numerous other national and local publications. He has been a consultant with the National Writing Project and has won two Educational Press Association of America awards for writing and editing. This is Mr. McPhee's second book. His first book, *AIDS,* was published by Grolier Publishing in 2000.

Mr. McPhee lives with his wife, Gay, and their children in Doylestown, Pennsylvania.